AMBIGUOUS CHILDHOODS

AMBIGUOUS CHILDHOODS

Peer Socialisation, Schooling and Agency in a
Zambian Village

Nana Clemensen

berghahn
NEW YORK · OXFORD
www.berghahnbooks.com

First published in 2019 by
Berghahn Books
www.berghahnbooks.com

© 2019, 2022 Nana Clemensen
First paperback edition published in 2022

Library of Congress Cataloging-in-Publication Data

Names: Clemensen, Nana, author.
Title: Ambiguous childhoods : peer socialisation, schooling and agency in a
 Zambian village / Nana Clemensen.
Description: New York : Berghahn Books, 2020. | Includes bibliographical
 references and index.
Identifiers: LCCN 2019026799 (print) | LCCN 2019026800 (ebook) | ISBN
 9781789203516 (hardback) | ISBN 9781789203523 (ebook)
Subjects: LCSH: Socialization--Zambia. | Social learning--Zambia. | Rural
 children--Zambia--Social conditions. | Children--Zambia--Social
 conditions. | Rural children--Education--Zambia. | Rural
 families--Zambia. | Social change--Zambia. | Zambia--Rural conditions.
Classification: LCC HQ792.Z33 C54 2020 (print) | LCC HQ792.Z33 (ebook) |
 DDC 305.23096894--dc23
LC record available at https://lccn.loc.gov/2019026799
LC ebook record available at https://lccn.loc.gov/2019026800

British Library Cataloguing in Publication Data

A catalogue record for this book is available from the British Library

ISBN 978-1-78920-351-6 hardback
ISBN 978-1-80073-432-6 paperback
ISBN 978-1-78920-352-3 ebook
https://doi.org/10.3167/9781789203516

✿ Contents

🌿 Acknowledgements

I wish to thank all children and adults in Hang'ombe Village who let me enter their lives and homes and allowed me to observe and record their most intimate conversations. Thank you also to all the unremitting teachers at Mbabala Basic School for opening their classrooms to me and sitting through repeated interviews. My deepest gratitude goes to 'my own' Hang'ombe family, whose warmth and generosity will remain with me forever: Benson, Sarah, Minivah, Khama, Talala, Mududu, Lushomo, Habeenzu and Lweendo; I dedicate this work to you.

More than anyone, I wish to thank my research assistant, colleague and friend Khama Hang'ombe, without whom this work would not have been possible. With his intelligence and commitment through more than ten years now, Khama has been a major influence on this work throughout all the stages of fieldwork and in later phases of translation and analysis.

In Lusaka, Professor Geofrey Tambulukani kept his office door open and gave valuable answers to my endless questions on school, children and family life. Professor Elizabeth Colson invited me and Khama into her Monze home and generously shared her immense knowledge about life and history among the Gwembe and Plateau Tonga.

In Denmark, I thank Danida and FFU for financing my studies and Iben Nørgaard for invaluable assistance to the administration of this work. I also wish to thank my colleagues at the Institute of Education (DPU) at Aarhus University for continuous inspiration and support. In particular, I thank my advisors Anne Holmen and Eva Gulløv for allowing and encouraging me to move along paths that I had not initially anticipated. Thanks to Christian Horst and Hanne Mogensen for important advice and feedback in the early stages of fieldwork – and to Lotte Meinert for directing my analyses later on. Special thanks to Kathryn Howard, Paul Wenzel Geissler, Karen Valentin and Elizabeth Colson for valuable feedback and suggestions. Thanks to my family and friends for helping me stay sane through the past few years of writing.

Finally, thanks to Berghahn Books for their patient guidance, and to the anonymous reviewers for their diligence and enthusiasm.

Nana Clemensen, Aarhus University, 2019

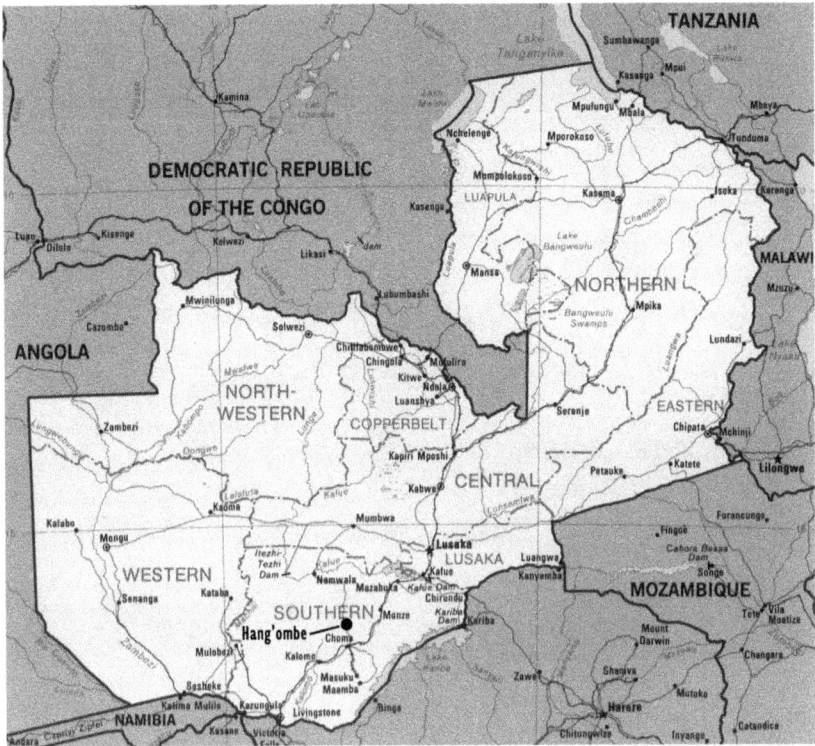

Map of Hang'ombe and the Mapanza Area. Library of Congress, Geography and Map Division, https://www.loc.gov/item/2001628307/.

The Mweemba homestead

Roy (M32), his wife Estar (F27) and their daughters Luyaba (F9) and Emma (F6).

Roy's brother Motty (M31), his wife Jackie (F28), their children Daala (M9), Disteria (F9), Munsanje (M7) and Edson (M6), along with Jackie's sister Frida (F10) and Motty's nephew Richwel (M9).

Roy and Motty's sister Irene (F33) and her children Brian (M9), Gary (M5) and John (M3).

Roy, Motty and Irene's parents Milo (M65) and Mairon (F63) and their nephew Alfred (M26).

The Hambuulo homestead

Levias (M38), his wife Lila (F32), and their four children Roy (M13), Oscar (M10), Luyando (F9) and Calleen (M7), plus their daughter Chipo (F17) who pursued secondary school in Choma.

The Phiri homestead

Shadrik (M48), his wife Love (F45), and their six children Mwiinga (F15), Julu (M11), Brenda (F9), Solomon (M9), Miyoba (F7) and Clever (M6), along with Love's granddaughters Malilwe (F11) and Shimbi (F6).

Love's nephew Obrian (M20), his wife Sarah (F18) and their newborn son Junior (M0).

Shadrik's aunt Elizabeth (F64) and her grandchildren Banda (M10), Nchimunya (M7) and Eden (F3).

The Hang'ombe homestead

Benson (M82), his wife Sarah (F67), Benson's daughter Minivah (F38) and her five children Talala (F11), Mududu (F9), Lushomo (F8), Habeenzu (M3) and Lweendo (F1), along with Benson's nephew Talis (M28), and his grandchildren Mutinta (F13) and Senefa (6).

Figure 0.1 The four Hang'ombe homesteads, divided into separate households (M=male, F=female).

❧ Introduction

GROWING UP IN HANG'OMBE VILLAGE

I stay quiet and listen closely whenever the adults speak.
—Brenda, 9-year-old girl

A good person talks, but not too much. There is some talk that is good and some that isn't. Nowadays, few people know the difference between the two.
—Minivah, 38-year-old mother of five

It was an afternoon in early January 2009 during the peak of the rainy season in Hang'ombe Village, a 40 km² cluster of rural homesteads among the Plateau Tonga of Zambia's Southern Province. Four children – 9-year-old Disteria, her brother Munsanje (7), their cousin Richwel (9) and their young aunt Frida (10) – walked along one of the paths traversing the area, each carrying a full water bucket on their head back to their mutual home of extended family members, referred to as the Mweemba *munzi* or homestead. The rains had been plenty this season, and so water could be found in the relative proximity of most homes. Frida had recently joined the homestead to assist her older sister Jackie – mother of Disteria and Munsanje and the paternal auntie of Richwel – as neither of Frida's parents had been able to take care of her after divorcing and remarrying. Richwel had been adopted by his aunt and uncle after his mother's death in 2002, and so he, Munsanje, Disteria and her twin brother Daala had grown up close together. Besides their household chores, all the children attended the local school, Mbabala Basic School, placed in the township about twenty minutes' walk from their home. Most Saturdays, the children visited the local Seventh Day Adventist church with their families, singing, preaching the gospel and joining the lively gatherings succeeding most meetings. This afternoon, like many others, the four children had gone to fetch water together, escaping the homestead for an hour while joking, singing, arguing, exchanging ideas and chatting about current events. As they walked back, Disteria invited them all to start singing together:[1]

1. Disteria: Tiye katuyabwiimba amutukke tweenda. [Singing] Hallelujah, hallelujah …

   Let's start off and sing as we move. [Singing] Hallelujah, hallelujah …

2. All the children [singing]: Alumbwe mwami wesu, alike akacinge bantu basyomeka. Hallelujah, hallelujah alike akacinge bantu basyomeka.

   Praise our God, He alone shall take the people who are faithful. Praise God, praise God, He alone shall take the people who are faithful.

3. Disteria: Wasika a chorus, mpoonya Frida, 'Hallelujah, hallelujah alumbwe mwami wesu'. Tiye 'Hallelujah, hallelujah alumbwe mwami wesu'.

   When we get to the chorus, you Frida should sing 'Hallelujah, hallelujah praise our God'. Let's sing 'Hallelujah, hallelujah praise our God'.

4. Frida [singing with Disteria]: Hallelujah.

   Hallelujah.

5. All the children [singing]: Hallelujah, hallelujah alumbwe mwami wesu, alike akacinge bantu basyomeka.

   Hallelujah, hallelujah praise our God, He alone shall take His faithful people.

[The singing ends. The children walk quietly for a while.]

6. Munsanje [to Disteria]: Mbomutisike buyo sena nkusamba?

   Immediately when you get home, will you take a bath?

7. Disteria: Ndaakusika nkuli tila-tila.

   Immediately when I get home, I'll take a quick bath.

8. Frida: Ndaakusika nkuli kupa buyo.

   When I get home, I [too] will take a quick bath.

9. Disteria: Mbonditikanjile buyo nkulicumba-cumba mweendo, nkusamba kumutwe nkuli kupa amubili.

> *Immediately when I get in the bathroom, I'll quickly wash my legs, wash my head and, in the end, the whole body.*

10. Frida [acknowledging]: Iiyi.

> *Yes.*

11. Disteria [to Frida]: Mulitila buyo? Kwamana mwanana mafwuta?

> *Do you just pour water on your body? After that [you] apply lotion?*

[Frida does not respond.]

12. Munsanje: Mebo inga nsesambi, alatontola meenda badaala.

> *I don't usually bathe, the water is very cold.*

13. Frida [to Munsanje, angrily]: Ndiyookwaamba! Ncocinunka dooti eci, ndiyookwaamba buya!

> *I'll report you! That's the reason you smell dirty, I'll definitely report you!*

14. Munsanje [angrily]: Ukaambe, ndiyookupwaya!

> *[If] you report me, I'll beat you!*

15. Disteria [to Munsanje]: Ukamupwaye kuli? Ncotasambi. Ndiyoobaambila ba auntie.

> *Why do you want to beat her? You don't bathe. I'll tell auntie.*

16. Richwel: Bayi besu balauma batasambi.

> *Our teacher beats those who don't bathe.*

17. Munsanje: Swebo tabaumi besu badaala. Ede inga taakwe ciindi cakusamba.

> *Our teacher doesn't beat. But I don't have time to bathe.*

This book explores the social lifeworlds of about twenty 6–12-year-old children living and growing up in the early twenty-first century in Hang'ombe Village, a rural chiTonga-speaking community in southern Zambia. Through nine months of linguistic-ethnographic fieldwork among four extended families in 2008–2009, along with a brief revisit in 2010, I have pursued the social experiences, practices and orientations displayed and expressed by these children in their everyday interactions, particularly among their siblings and kin. As in many parts of rural Africa (Nsamenang 2008), Hang'ombe children grow up in close-knit, multigenerational subsistence farm-based homesteads to which they are expected to contribute from around the age of five, gradually taking on more demanding household chores and responsibilities. Unlike in highly industrialised societies dominated by single-family households and age-segregated childcare systems, children in rural African communities tend to be surrounded by other children of a wide age spectrum throughout their days, including siblings, cousins and extended family members living within or in close distance of their home. The close composition of Hang'ombe homesteads allows parents to entrust older children – their own or extended family members – with the care of toddlers and leave them out of direct adult supervision for several hours a day. Adult family members sometimes assist if the older children are away for school or errands, but by the age of 4–5 years, children are left to roam around in the vicinity of homesteads more or less on their own, providing them with a degree of physical freedom unfamiliar to most children growing up in Western societies today.

As apparent in the extract with Disteria and her peers above, Hang'ombe boys and girls sought to perform many of their daily chores together: fetching water, herding goats, chopping vegetables or picking fruits. Work and play were often intertwined, and adults interfered little with children's organisation of activities as long as they did their chores. The sibling-kin group thus formed a significant unit of children's basic socialisation, allowing them to explore and process the social information gained from different domains of daily life. Varying in age, gender and affinity, such groups provided children with multiple roles and relationships, like ally, caretaker, teacher and authority, creating a relatively safe space for their mutual investigation of the world around them. The intimacy of the homestead and the conduct of household chores gave them close exposure to the lives and concerns of older family members. Much of this exposure remained implicit – that is, without adults' direct clarification – as children were largely expected to remain quiet and attentive in the company of elders, including parents. Out of adults' earshot, however, children could be found chattering intensely with their siblings and peers, examining and creatively employing various kinds of social information available to them. To the interested observer, such chatter may serve as a dense source of insight into children's everyday lives and experiences in a contemporary rural African society.

Changing Family Lives

Hang'ombe Village constituted a 40km^2 cluster of eighty-two homesteads, placed in the Mapanza District at the lower centre of Zambia's Southern Province. Each homestead was surrounded by maize fields and large bush areas kept uncultivated mainly for the grazing of cattle. Varying widely from one member to several generations cohabiting, these homesteads accommodated around 300 people between the ages of 0–93, most of whom were interrelated through marriage or kin. Referred to in the anthropological literature as the Plateau Tonga (Lancaster and Vickery 2007), the large majority were chiTonga speakers and identified as being Tongas prior to the more abstract category of 'Zambian' (Posner 2005). This also showed linguistically (although many people had at least some proficiency in English), with Zambia's main lingua francae, chiBemba and chiNyanja, communicated almost solely in chiTonga, also when speaking with teachers, nurses, veterinarians or other formally educated personnel. English remained the language of national matters as displayed on radio and TV, in higher administrative offices and, in particular, formal education (Spitulnik 1998).

Practically all families were sustained by farming and cattle herding, and throughout the planting and harvesting seasons from October to early May, men and women spent at least part of their days working in the maize fields, often assisted by their children. Socio-economic differences existed that were primarily centred on sizes of land and livestock and, increasingly, around adult children's level of formal education and employment, but these differences were relatively minor in the face of daily concerns. In the past few decades, life in the village had been challenged by periods of drought and cattle disease, rising fertiliser prices and, perhaps more than anything, the advent of HIV/Aids. On a more immediate scale, economic instability formed the daily organisation of family life, along with the shifting fads of local political powers. While Zambia's national economy had grown rapidly from around 2000 after decades of steep decline, agriculture remained stagnant throughout the region (Resnick and Thurlow 2014), and many farmers struggled to feed their families. Basic tasks like selling vegetables at the market or taking an aging father to the hospital were subject to rather unpredictable circumstances, like heavy rains or the whims of a car-owning relative. Formal jobs were scarce, transient and low paid, like roadwork, revenue collection, or tobacco-handling at local industrial farms. Some villagers ran successful businesses, vending cell phones and household items in small shops, while others sold the products of a thriving garden to bus passengers passing through town. But most considered themselves poor, unable to obtain the living conditions they desired for themselves and their families.

As Tongas, most families were matrilineally associated, identifying primarily with their maternal relatives, and children of both genders were generally seen as adhering to their mother's relatives also after the payment of full bride price or *lobola*. At the same time, Hang'ombe was a highly patriarchal society, with few women owning land or sustaining their own income, although some, mostly older women, managed the cultivation and sales of vegetables from their own gardens (Cliggett 2000; Mizinga 2000). Most women moved to their husband's homestead when marrying and returned to their father's land if divorcing. Women and girls managed the majority of housework, and while men performed strenuous seasonal chores in the homestead and maize fields, like construction, repairment, ploughing and reaping, they generally possessed more social and physical freedom than women. Girls were assigned with increasingly demanding household chores from the age of five, and while their brothers and male cousins might accompany them, as we saw in the initial example, boys were largely given much more leeway than girls. Such gendered distinctions were sustained by families' strong concern with the moral reputation of young girls, promoting ideals of servility and modesty much more adamantly for girls than boys.

While many aspects of daily life resembled that of people living in the area prior to Zambia's independence in 1964, Hang'ombe Village was in a state of ongoing social change. At school, teachers encouraged both male and female students to postpone childbirth and marriage and pursue further education, prompting their aspirations of professional careers and material wealth. Attracted by the commodified lifestyles they were exposed to in towns and the media, young men and women increasingly sought employment in urban centres, abandoning traditional trades and deeds of village life. Most parents and grandparents supported such chances of economic advance, but they also feared that youngsters' increasing mobility and independence might threaten the intergenerational contract and moral coherence among family members. At the same time, many elders regretted their inability to help children reach a viable pathway in life, as neither farming nor commerce seemed to offer them profitable careers. Basic family structures were thus in flux, increasing conflicts and uncertainties for some while enabling new roles and possibilities for others. Different notions of tradition and modernity imbued local world views, reflecting mixed experiences and expectations of societal change.

Traversed by the major connecting artery Namwala Road, most homesteads were placed in short walking distance of Mbabala Township, a peri-urban community of about 1,200 inhabitants, hosting a school, a council, a clinic, a marketplace, a few NGO representatives, a police station and a number of tailors, shops and bars. To villagers, the township contained both the promises and pitfalls of modern life. Parents complained about their children's exposure to 'bad behaviours' (*kubula ciimo*) – that is, the flows of alcohol, *dagga* (marihuana), South African TV stations and loud hip-hop music available in the township, widely associated with urban youth culture in Africa and the West. At the same time, the township represented progress and promises of a more comfortable life. The marketplace, established by a union of local farmers in the late 1990s, had become a source of income for many families, with women overseeing the money they earned from selling maize, cabbage and fruits grown in their private gardens. Trucks and buses loaded with travellers between the larger towns of Choma and Namwala ensured a continuous stream of customers for these women, especially after the road's long-awaited tarring in 2010. Nurses, social workers, veterinarians and school teachers present in the township were regarded with admiration and secret envy. With their electrified houses, expensive-looking clothes and sophisticated speech, these people impersonated concepts of schooling and modernity among villagers, most of whom had low education levels themselves. The township's educational establishments – including centres of adult literacy, crafts education and, notably, the local school – were seen as markers of progress for the entire community.

Mbabala Basic School

Placed on the outskirts of the township, Mbabala Basic School covered the schooling of children both within Mbabala and a number of surrounding villages. After the introduction of universal primary education in the late 1990s, most children in the area entered school around the age of seven, and although one or both their parents might also have spent at least a couple of years in school, the matter of course with which boys and girls were sent to school in 2008 was quite new. Many people had mixed feelings towards the local school, at once praising and questioning its ability to provide long-term benefits – further education and/or paid employment – for students and their families. As noted above, such feelings were particularly pronounced around the continued schooling of young girls, with modern schools encouraging both male and female students to postpone childbirth and marriage beyond their completion of grade twelve (Johnson-Hanks 2006; Stambach 2000). Although most adults in Hang'ombe supported the schooling of their daughters, nieces and granddaughters, many criticised local teachers for instilling them with unrealistic and immoral ideas of a modern, independent life in the city, far away from the daily chores of village life.

While the idea of formal education was surrounded by an almost mythological realm, children's contributions to the sustenance of households and fields were thus generally given much higher priority by local families than their absorption in school-related activities like reading or writing homework. Many parents complained about recurrently having to pay for children's notebooks, pens, uniforms and 'extra lessons', which formed large expenses for most families – and teachers told me how, in spite of their urgent appeals to parents about assisting with the construction of a new classroom building, very few had indeed shown up. These tendencies, rather than revealing villagers' 'bad morals' as some teachers put it to me, might reflect a deep-rooted scepticism towards schooling and its capacity to redeem its promises of a better future for children and their families alike. In spite of gradually increasing enrolment and graduation levels, unemployment in the area remained high, and access to secondary and, in particular, higher education was limited for most youngsters. As noted above, many parents viewed social conduct in the township as a tangible threat to the moral cohesion of families, a concern that the school was unable to soothe in spite of weekly lessons of Moral Education in higher grades. Teachers were respected while at the same time distrusted for their inability to provide children with better futures. As I discuss further on, many Hang'ombe children displayed mixed attitudes towards schooling in line with their parents, perhaps perceiving its ambiguous connotations in local society.

Moral Ambiguities

Like school, the church held a central symbolic space among villagers. Most people considered themselves devoted Christians, frequenting either the Seventh Day Adventist Church (about 70%) or another congregation in the area: Brethren in Christ Church, Nazareen Church,

Roman Catholic Church, New Apostolic Church, Zionist Church or the Church of Jehovah's Witnesses. Men and women sat in separate rows while children ran in and out, playing and chatting with their friends. From around the age of five, many children frequented either a Sabbath or Sunday school, learning Biblical parables and songs. Like school, the church institutionalised ideals of pristinity and righteousness, and like teachers, church elders were respected and feared for their knowledge and literary skills. Phrases like 'God is great' (*Mwami mupati*) and 'worshiping [God] is good' (*kukomba ncibotu*) permeated colloquial speech in many homes, and social conduct was widely assessed by reference to the decora promoted by preachers, like verbal 'softness', generosity, diligence, sobriety, monogamy and sexual moderation.

At the same time, the frequency with which such decora were discussed in local homes also revealed their difficult compatibility with the hardships and temptations of daily life. With sparse food reserves and large families, people did not always act as generously towards their neighbours during periods of starvation or drought as urged to by local preachers, and theft formed an increasing problem across households. Some men went straight to one of the township taverns after finishing their work in the fields, drinking and playing cards, just as some women with tight budgets offered sexual services against payment from well-off, mostly married men, particularly in the township, where chances of meeting non-locals were high. As noted earlier, children's relatively free access to most arenas of daily life provided them with close exposure to the varying, sometimes conflicting terms of adult life. Depending on their level of maturity, children might not fully understand such conflict, as adults rarely offered much explanation. Instead, children used their peers – especially siblings and cousins with whom they spent most of their time outside classrooms – processing, negotiating and creatively appropriating the social knowledge presented to them, gradually producing their own interpretations of the world around them. Centring on such peer interactions and their active interplay with different levels of adult exposure, I argue that children in rural majority settings like Hang'ombe Village acquire an advanced social and linguistic competence highly relevant not only to their present-day lives but also to their potential futures in a fluctuating society. This approach is informed by a number of theoretical strands, which I introduce below.

Children's Sibling and Kin Cultures

In spite of their prevalence and social significance, especially in rural societies across the majority world, relatively few studies have explored the social dynamics of children's sibling-kin groups ethnographically. One reason may be that such groups often speak in languages that may be unfamiliar to the great majority of social scientists. As childhood sociologist William Corsaro writes,

> We know much less about the nature and complexity of children's peer cultures in non-western societies [than in western societies] for a variety of reasons. First, most of the research focuses on children's psychological development rather than the nature of their childhoods and peer cultures. Secondly, children in non-western societies often live challenging lives due to poverty and political instability and often enter the adult world of work at an early age. Research on children in these circumstances is more applied and focuses on documenting the poor conditions of children's lives and developing programs and policies to provide them education and opportunities to have some degree of a childhood … Thirdly, the dominance of the English language in the world (especially the western academic world) means that many studies and reports of children's lives in non-western societies are not known beyond a particular society or group of societies which share the particular or a similar language. (Corsaro 2009: 308)

Exceptions to this lacuna do exist, however, including ethnographic studies of children's peer and sibling cultures in sub-Saharan Africa. As examples, social psychologist A. Bame Nsamenang has produced a contextually rich literature on patterns of children's socialisation and development prevailing in mid and late twentieth century rural Africa, based on extensive ethnography primarily among Nso children's sibling-kin groups in northern Cameroon (Nsamenang 1992, 2008; Nsamenang and Lamb 1994). Anthropologist David Lancy has explored Kpelle children's self-generated play practices in rural Liberia through thirty years of study, including role play, structured games, songs and storytelling (Lancy 1996, 2015). Geographer Cindi Katz has described Howa children's closely intertwined work and play practices among their siblings and peers in eastern Sudan, analysing the repercussions of broader economic, cultural and political changes on children's lives and potential futures in local society (Katz 2004, 2012). More recently, literary ethnographer Tadesse Jaleta Jirata has pursued Guji children's creative use of traditional riddles in rural Ethiopia, displaying how children thus acquire vital cultural information and establish their own identities and self-expressions in local society (Jirata 2012). Varying in regional and theoretical scope, these ethnographies show the societal significance of sibling-kin groups to children's basic socialisation, learning and identity formation in contemporary rural Africa, where children spend many of their waking hours unattended by adults.

In Hang'ombe, children's immediate relationships mostly pertained to the homestead and the surrounding fields and gardens, where they spent large parts of their day in the company of different relatives. Children also had more or less stable relationships with classmates, teachers, church elders, neighbours and extended relatives, with whom they interacted in different arenas like the church, the classroom, the township and the homestead, each presenting children with slightly different norms and possibilities. In line with current childhood sociology, I assume all of these relationships and arenas to hold potential influence on the socialisation and basic life experiences of boys and girls, including their own role(s) and ways of navigating in that world. I further assume that children take on varying subject positions, enabling them to reinterpret the various practices and ideologies available to them in accordance with their personal interests and concerns (e.g. Corsaro 2009). As noted earlier, this assumption departs from early understandings of children's socialisation (e.g. Mead 1928; Whiting and Whiting 1975), many of which approached children as miniature adults and their socialisation as a linear, predictable process, tied to older family members' practices and ideals. Child anthropologist Christina Toren has noted how such understandings fail to account for children's ongoing manipulation of the symbolic categories and practices available to them:

> It makes no sense to dismiss children's ideas as immature, or to argue that they do not understand what is really going on. Children have to live their lives in terms of their understandings, just as adults do; their ideas are grounded in their experience and thus equally valid. The challenge for the anthropologist is to analyse the processes that make it possible for children to lead effective lives in terms of ideas that are an inversion of those held by their parents and other adults. (Toren 1993: 463)

To make qualified assumptions about children's experiences of the world around them, we must investigate their conduct on their own premises – that is, their personal experiences, relationships, desires and fears. The actions and orientations of parents and other adult figures obviously affect children's lives, enhancing particular experiences while restricting others – perhaps especially in a society where children's lives are closely intertwined with the activities of family members. Children have fewer life experiences to rely on than adults, and so they observe the routines of older members while learning and establishing their own roles in the world around them. They notice the validity ascribed to different practices, seeing how certain behaviours evoke positive or negative, strong or indifferent reactions, and they try out some of these behaviours and their social impact among peers. Hang'ombe children were generally placed at the lower end of social hierarchy, and so their experience and interpretation of the world around them was marked by certain restrictions and duties, many of which were 'boring, burdensome, or unpleasant', as observed among Beti children in southern Cameroon (Johnson-Hanks 2006: 54). But this subordinate position also allowed children certain privileges, letting them pass relatively unnoticed through daily village life.

Peer Socialisation Studies

As a growing segment of childhood sociology and anthropology, the linguistic-anthropological paradigm of *language socialisation studies* has made significant contributions on the tangible routines and conditions comprising different childhood experiences. Since its initiation by child anthropologists in the 1980s (Schieffelin and Ochs 1986), the paradigm has pursued the cultural premises for children's – and other novices' – acquisition of and participation in the social practices, knowledge and orientations prevailing in particular societies and settings, like homes, day-care facilities, schools and workplaces, in different parts of the world. Language socialisation scholars have shown the basic significance of *language* in this process, drawing on extensive linguistic-ethnographic studies of everyday interactions among children, their caretakers and teachers. In the past two decades, language socialisation scholars have paid increasing interest to children's interactions with *peers*, unsolicited or at least not directly modified by adults (Cekaite et al. 2014; Goodwin and Kyratzis 2012). Approaching children's peer cultures as marked by their own distinct social routines, interpretive frames and linguistic codes – changing as children grow cognitively and linguistically more adept – this research displays children's complex discursive competences when talking, playing or arguing with their siblings, classmates and friends. Cekaite et al. describe how children's peer cultures may be seen as independent, highly creative appropriations of the social and discursive orders prevailing around them, informing children's identity formation among their peers as well as in their wider social communities:

[T]here is a dialectic, mutually informing, relation between children's and adults' cultures: it is through the processes of 'creative appropriation', 'interpretive reproduction' and even 'secondary adjustments' (e.g. subversive practices, Goffman 1967 cf. Blum-Kulka et al. 2004) that children explore, are socialized, and take their own stance on adult practices, and that they, over time, become part of a dynamically shaped adult culture, acquiring or transforming adult-like communicative competences and resources. Children in peer activities can be seen to both appropriate and reinterpret adult practices and resources in ways that make them peer specific. (Cekaite et al. 2014: 6)

Although predominantly conducted in Western societies, an increasing number of peer socialisation studies have explored children's lifeworlds in majority settings, often centring on children's playful interactions with their siblings and kin: Laurence R. Goldman has analysed how Huli children in Papua New Guinea evoke and actively interplay with local cosmologies and narrative conventions in their peer activities of pretence play (Goldman 1998). Amanda Minks has depicted a sibling-kin group of 7–12-year-old Miskitu children in eastern Nicaragua creatively combining features from different linguistic registers associated with a powerful elite, like teacher talk and media discourse, thus positioning themselves as competent, autonomous actors in the local social order (Minks 2006, 2008, 2010, 2013). Jennifer Reynolds has revealed how kin-related Mayan children in Guatemala negotiate and sometimes subvert existing power relations through the playful use of different linguistic genres, routines and registers commonly associated with adult authoritative figures, like the greeting *'Buenos días'* combined with a military salute (Reynolds 2007), the Spanish reconquest genre *El Desafío* (Reynolds 2010) and local, historically anchored expressions of social delinquency and lynching (Reynolds 2013). Amy Paugh's decade-long studies among young siblings and kin-related peers on the Caribbean island of Dominica (Paugh 2005, 2012) have shown children's central role in the ongoing national language shift, a process charged with complex historical issues of identity, power, resistance and change. Camilla Rindstedt has illustrated how young Quichua siblings on the Ecuadorian sierra play with prevailing power structures between indigenous people and the mestizos, mimicking the linguistic registers of both authoritative and subordinate adult figures (Rindstedt 2001; Rindstedt and Aronsson 2002). Lourdes de León has explored a group of young siblings' interactions in Chiapas, Mexico, describing their linguistically subtle, ongoing negotiations of age-based roles and hierarchies, mimicking and subverting the registers and routines of adults around them (De León 2007, 2009, 2015, 2018). Flores Nájera has studied bilingual, Nahuatl-Spanish-speaking children in Tlaxcala, Mexico, revealing the older children's strategic use of code-switching and honorific forms towards their younger siblings during play (Nájera 2009). Kathryn Howard's studies of young rural children in northern Thailand (Howard 2007, 2009a, 2009b) have revealed children's participation in the ongoing language shift between the vernacular Kam Muang and Standard Thai, positioning themselves against the puritanical demands of both parents and teachers and creating their own syncretic variety.

These peer socialisation studies all reveal children's active roles in processes of societal reproduction and change, interacting with local family systems, power relations, linguistic ideologies, economic and educational structures etc. Perhaps more than Western societies, societies in the majority world tend to undergo sociocultural and economic changes in rapid, uneven ways, evoking a particular need for new interpretations of current realities. Children produce such interpretations in the relative experimental freedom of the peer group, making it a potent arena for studying both immediate and larger societal themes. Ethnographic childhood studies reveal broad cultural and linguistic varieties in children's lifeworlds, but they also show generic patterns of intimacy and dispute, social adaptability and creativity – qualities that may be socially and emotionally enhanced in the shared horizon of close-knit rural societies in the majority world in which most children rely heavily on each other's attention and support.

Inspired by peer socialisation studies' close ethnographic, agency-oriented research approach to children's lives and practices in everyday life, the current study gives both empirical and analytical prominence to children's verbal interactions with peers and other central actors around them and the personal perspectives these interactions may reveal. Grounded in the field of linguistic anthropology, peer socialisation studies produce detailed analyses of the distinctive linguistic features of children's peer interactions, revealing their creative use and growing mastery of different linguistic means and registers available to them. Such close attention to linguistic detail allows for the tangible scrutiny of complex social and developmental processes, like children's active acquisition of specific cultural knowledge. However, linguistic analyses may often appear somewhat inaccessible to non-linguist readers, in spite of shared interests in themes of, for example, childhood, identity, socialisation and schooling. With the aim of addressing a broad readership of students, scholars and practitioners, the analyses of this book generally centre more on *what* Hang'ombe children talk about (and also what they omit talking about) in certain situations than on *how* they talk about it. Obviously, such distinction between linguistic form and content has long been dismissed by modern sociolinguistics, demonstrating their inseparability in authentic human interaction (Hymes 1967). But whereas language socialisation and peer socialisation studies generally focus on children's acquisition of specific linguistic formats (Kulick and Schieffelin 2004), my analyses focus more broadly on Hang'ombe children's experiences and appropriations of the cultural knowledge and conventions presented to them, including locally significant linguistic registers. As such, the book might be classified as intersecting social and linguistic anthropology, employing extracts of Hang'ombe children and adults' everyday talk as micro-ethnographic entries into the different social arenas that the children inhabit and co-produce. Drawing on a spectrum of childhood and Africanist studies, the book's analyses entail wider discussions of children's roles and perspectives in a changing majority world society, as I elaborate below.

Exploring 'the African Child'

Recent ethnographies have avoided prevailing tendencies to either victimise or romanticise the 'African child', instead bringing out more diverse, experience-based accounts of children growing up in various parts and strata of contemporary Africa (e.g. Abebe and Ofosu-Kusi 2016; Christiansen, Utas and Vigh 2006; Ensor 2012; Honwana and De Boeck 2005; Spittler and Bourdillon 2012). Common to these accounts is a focus on children's integral roles and complex agencies in local African communities of various kinds, 'theoriz[ing] how children, through their engagements in the social, economic, cultural and political life of their societies, contribute to the reconfiguration of social and generational dynamics unfolding in their societies' (Abebe and Ofosu-Kusi 2016: 305). While acknowledging the prevalence of political and economic challenges across the African continent, affecting the lives of adults, youths and children alike, these scholars underline the need for studies of more nuanced and mundane everyday experiences among African children, including play and leisure activities. Rather than reinforce the 'othering' and homogenisation of African identities common to media, political and research discourse throughout the past century, we should study the increasing implications of globally and world-historically constructed ideas; for example, on childhood, education, work and family life in Africa, as in any other part of the contemporary world (Abebe and Ofosu-Kusi 2016; Imoh 2016). The central actors of this book are based in an African village, a setting approached by countless anthropologists and historians throughout the past century. However, accentuating children's own interactions and accounts – primarily with their siblings and kin but also with their parents, grandparents, teachers and other adult figures – I seek to rework stereotypical images of both 'the African village' and 'the African child'. Implementing broad-scale theories of uncertainty and post-colonialism to the ethnographic paradigms of childhood sociology and peer language socialisation studies, I analyse the children's creative interactions with both local and global conditions in their daily social practices, containing both common and quite particular childhood experiences.

Lived Uncertainties

I thus combine close analysis of children's peer cultures and interactions with broader patterns in their daily lives in a rural African society, including aspects of class, gender, schooling, religion and generational and political changes. Contextualising such insights, I draw on prominent anthropological theories on life, sociality and intimacy in contemporary Africa, most of which explore *uncertainty* as a productive, indispensable living condition. In the past decade, such theories have allowed a rethinking of conventional 'development'-oriented research, enabling a literature more closely tied to people's subjective experiences, dilemmas, actions and aspirations (e.g. Cliggett et al. 2007; Cooper and Pratten 2015; Haram and Yamba 2009). Approaching uncertainty as 'a structure of feeling – the lived experience of a pervasive sense of vulnerability, anxiety, hope, and possibility mediated through the material assemblages that underpin, saturate, and sustain everyday life' (Cooper and Pratten 2015: 1), this literature reveals the often advanced strategies employed by individuals living in constantly shifting contexts of social interdependence, climatic changes and political and economic instabilities. As examples, Jennifer Johnson-Hanks describes the judicious pregnancy planning among educated Beti women in southern Cameroon, balancing a complex moral economy between local honour systems and the contradictory demands of modern schooling in what she calls *vital conjunctures* (Johnson-Hanks 2006). Susan Whyte and Godfrey E. Siu explore Ugandan HIV patients' vigilant management of what the authors refer to as social and historical *contingencies* in order to ensure medical treatment and create better lives for themselves (Whyte and Siu 2015). Peter Geschiere depicts the witchcraft practices thriving across contemporary Africa as a logical, highly modern response to what he refers to as the fundamental *ambiguity of intimacy*, offering both solace and potential deceit (Geschiere 2013).

Compared to some parts of contemporary Africa, a Zambian village like Hang'ombe might offer children relative stability in terms of food, housing, family care, access to medication and schooling – but experiences of uncertainty and ambiguity also prevail in this part of the continent, affecting children and adults alike. Families' general vulnerability towards climatic and economic fluctuations urges children to remain alert and industrious and to adopt changing living standards and family compositions as some members leave and others arrive. Different and sometimes contradictory conventions prevail in different social arenas, inciting children to manoeuvre in flexible and often creative ways. On a wider scale, fluctuating global markets and trends affect children's future horizons as conceived by themselves, their teachers and caretakers, revealing new possibilities along with sudden risks and restraints.

In his book *Expectations of Modernity: Myths and Meanings of Urban Life on the Zambian Copperbelt*, anthropologist James Ferguson explores the sociocultural and psychological repercussions of the radical societal changes marking Zambia's more recent history (Ferguson 1999). Through the narrated life experiences of mine workers in the Zambian Copperbelt, he unfolds the post-independent euphoria and rapid infrastructural development of the late 1960s, the steep economic decline and despair following the global copper crisis in the mid 1970s and the subsequent decades of struggle among large parts of the population to re-create not only a physical livelihood but also a revised sense of self. From modern cosmopolitans and world citizens, many Zambians now had to adopt a more humble self-image and existence, often involving the re-establishment of strained kinship relations and responsibilities (Ferguson 1999: 123ff). Zambia's economic situation has gradually changed since, but the *crisis of meaning* called out by Ferguson and others (Crehan 1997; Ferguson 1999: 14; Moore and Vaughan 1994) seems to have endured, visible, for example, in the high unemployment rate prevailing especially in Zambia's urban areas (World Bank 2013) and the increasing hardships among young men both in rural and urban areas to provide for a wife and children, let alone their aging parents (Cliggett 2005). In a study on relations between urban space, socio-economic mobility and gender in the lives of adolescents in Lusaka, anthropologist Karen Tranberg Hansen suggests that many young Zambians – especially men – now struggle to attain the economic status and independence necessary for them to be recognised as adults, not only by older generations but also among themselves (Hansen 2005). Confronted with alluring global media discourses of their 'potential as the leaders of tomorrow' (Hansen 2005: 13), as well as with the local realities of global neoliberalism – that is, increased social and economic uncertainty, inequality and exclusion (Hansen 2005: 4) – the young people in Hansen's study express the literal and metaphorical challenge of being 'stuck in the compound', unable to transcend the social and economic constraints associated with being young and poor.

Although Ferguson and Hansen's studies were both conducted in urban areas in the 1990s, the crisis of meaning they address also concerns the generations of Zambians currently living in rural communities like Hang'ombe. The families I observed all conveyed fundamental experiences of uncertainty, not just physically and financially – southern Zambia had been struck by cattle decease and severe drought in the past decade, affecting livestock and maize, two dominant sources of food and income in the region – but also experiences of devastating social change, like a weakening of kinship ties and intergenerational reciprocity, a disbelief in the capacities of schooling and increasing cases of theft, violence and alcoholism. My study pursues Hang'ombe children's various ways of encountering and dealing with such uncertainty, primarily through the ethnographic lens provided by social interactions with their siblings and kin, like the extract at the outset of this chapter to which I now return.

Appropriating Adult Discourse

In the extract at the beginning of this chapter, 9-year-old Disteria, her brother Munsanje (7), their cousin Richwel (9), and their young aunt Frida (10) were depicted in the middle of an ongoing interaction as they were walking the approximately 5 km back and forth to the village well from their mutual homestead. Slightly more confident and verbally adept than her peers, Disteria dominated much of this interaction, perhaps incited by the fact that I had asked her to keep the digital recorder in her front pocket this afternoon. As the extract begins, Disteria initiates the group's collective singing of the hymn *'Hallelujah, alumbwe mwami wesu'* (Hallelujah, praise Our God), imitating the oratorical style of local preachers at the weekly sermons (line 1). Her three peers immediately join in (line 2), seemingly familiar with the hymn from church and most likely also from home. The Adventist Church held a strong social and symbolic role among all the families I observed, including the Mweemba's, and collective singing was common, especially among women working or walking together in fields and households. Young girls often sang with their mothers or older sisters in the gardens, shifting between voices and enabling both a spiritual and social communion among them. Disteria's call may be seen as inviting a similar communion among her peers but also as her active appropriation of a sophisticated practice like the part-singing of Christian hymns, interplaying with common ideals and modes of self-expression. When talking with peers, boys and girls often evoked the symbols and practices of church – singing, quoting the Bible or mimicking the grave voice and dramatic gestures and register common to local preachers.

As their singing ends, Disteria and her peers start talking about personal hygiene, sharing their routines and frequencies of bathing (lines 6–17) – practices that among most families indicated a person's level of social decency. Munsanje asks if Disteria is going to bathe as they return from their long walk (line 6) – perhaps airing his own aversion to bathing, which had already been subject to some dispute among them earlier on. Disteria and Frida both confirm this question (lines 7–8), Disteria keenly elaborating that 'Immediately when I get in the bathroom, I will quickly wash my legs, wash my head and, in the end, the whole body' (line 9). She asks Frida if she is as meticulous in her bathing as herself, or if she just 'pours water on her body' (line 10), a question Frida does not answer. Such concern with the details of personal hygiene, dress and appearance was often expressed among girls and women, especially young teenagers whose preparation for marital eligibility had begun. Mothers urged their daughters and sons to wash frequently and wear clean, presentable clothes whenever they were not busy working, and members of all ages dressed immaculately – and expensively – for the weekly sermons. The children's interest in each other's bathing routines may reflect such parental concerns but can also be seen as their appropriation of a powerful moral discourse, prevalent in local preachers' talk of cleanliness (*bulondo*) as a Christian virtue and in teachers' promotion of a modern, civilised lifestyle. Challenging the authority of such discourse, Munsanje notes: 'I don't usually bathe, the water is very cold' (line 12). This upsets Frida, who threatens him with report (line 13), most likely to his mother Jackie, the female authority of their mutual home – but Munsanje does not subside, instead threatening to beat her (line 14). Disteria now interferes, asking Munsanje matter-of-factly why he wants to beat Frida when she is simply telling the truth – and then repeats Frida's threat to 'tell auntie' (line 15). 9-year-old Richwel then evokes the school's moral authority, saying 'Our teacher beats those who don't bathe' (line 16). Munsanje responds 'Our teacher doesn't beat' (line 17), cleverly questioning Richwel's claim rather than defending his own bathing aversion. Corporal punishment had been contested and prohibited among Mbabala teachers in recent years, following national campaigns and a gradual change in attitude towards children's education across homes and schools. However, some teachers were known to threaten or give students an occasional beating if provoked. Munsanje thus elicits wider themes of modern and traditional authority informing different aspects of the children's lives. He then adds 'But I don't have time to bathe' (line 17), underlining his wilful position against such authorities.

The interaction between Munsanje, Disteria, Frida and Richwel depicts a widespread concern among the Hang'ombe children I observed with the social and moral discourses of the institutions dominating their lives: teacher talk and school regulations in and out of classrooms, preacher conduct and church etiquette, parental directives and rebukes – all were vehemently discussed and appropriated in creative ways, often testing or challenging prevailing norms and hierarchies, like in the latter part of the children's talk above. Negotiating social and moral orders across households, the children sought to build favourable positions for themselves among peers, gradually developing their own social and discursive skills.

Composition of the Book

Exploring Hang'ombe children's interactions with their immediate social environments, mostly at home and at school, the book's chapters are built around extracts of everyday talk among children, their peers and caretakers, selected from a large corpus of ethnographic observations and digital sound recordings. Like Corsaro, I approach the children as active, collective producers of peer cultures constantly interacting with factors prevailing both within and beyond the constraints of the peer or kin-sibling group, including the adults around them (Corsaro 2009). In line with peer language socialisation studies, I illustrate how Hang'ombe children use their peer interactions not only to explore and reproduce the ambiguous social order prevailing around them but also to negotiate and sometimes subvert this order, building alignments and positions for themselves and each other both within and beyond the peer group. Following current trends in child anthropology (James and Prout 1997; Qvortrup et al. 2009), I approach the children as relatively independent actors, possessing their own agencies, interests and interpretations of the social and institutional arenas in which they take part while at the same time depending on such arenas.

In Chapter 1, I review the volatile undertaking of fieldwork underlying this work and the sequence of events leading to its final shape. I introduce the members of the four homesteads participating in the study and reflect upon my own positionality as a white educated woman. I discuss my own and my research assistant Khama Hang'ombe's increasing attention to children's peer interactions and consider ethical and methodological issues associated with this approach, including ethnographic work among minors and the use of local interpreters. Finally, I present my considerations on the transcription and presentation of data in this book.

In Chapter 2, I explore the basic routines and relationships framing Hang'ombe children's early socialisation, closely tied to the sustenance of families and the close interdependency between family and community members. Drawing on sociocultural learning theories, I present the socio-affective ideals underlying children's participation in the endeavours of older family members and the sometimes conflicting interests and uncertainties appearing among family members living in a changing society. Lastly, I discuss the social implications of children's relatively unimpeded access to the concerns and moral ambiguities of adult life, which they are exposed to in different arenas; for example, in the local township and in the lively talk around family fires at night.

In Chapter 3, I explore children's responses to the various kinds of social information available to them in daily life, focusing on their interactions with siblings and kin. Drawing on peer language socialisation studies, I illustrate children's creative and sometimes subversive appropriation of prevailing power structures and discuss the social and educational aspects of such appropriation.

In Chapter 4, I investigate the tangible and symbolic domain of schooling, analysing classroom practices and ideologies as it might be experienced by Hang'ombe children. From there, I return to households and discuss the ambiguities of schooling as a powerful, yet precarious enterprise. Extending from Chapter 3, I continue to analyse children's creative use of academic discourse in their peer interactions, thus challenging prevailing stereotypes of rural African children as uneducated or deprived.

Finally, in the Conclusion, I reflect upon some of the participating children's current life situations, especially in terms of schooling. Resuming from the initial chapter, I discuss the book's depictions of daily community life and concerns in the light of fundamental uncertainties, along with historical events preceding current life circumstances among the Plateau Tongas. I summarise the distinct learning trajectories and communicative practices adopted by Hang'ombe children and discuss, briefly, how such trajectories and practices might be sustained and utilised more constructively in formal education.

Note

1. Disteria held the recorder, recording herself and her peers for a few hours.

❧ 1

APPROACHING CHILDREN'S PERSPECTIVES
Reflections on Fieldwork

> Whatever you say, [the recorder] records. Even if you make an insult, it will record.
> —Luyaba, 9-year-old girl

> Nobody has ever asked me questions like these before. But since you are asking me things which I know very well, I can easily explain.
> —Benson, 82-year-old former headman, father and grandfather of 20+ children

When I first arrived in Zambia in early 2008, I had only a vague conception of the fieldwork I would undertake over the coming year. I knew I was going to look at language practices and early education, particularly mother tongue education, which had gained increasing attention among national and international stakeholders in African education, including the Danish aid agency financing my studies. My main contact in Zambia was a professor at the School of Education in Lusaka, Geofrey Tambulukani, who had been involved in both the planning and national implementation of the mother-tongue based Primary Reading Programme, which had recently gained international acclaim (Sampa 2003; 2005). On Tambulukani's suggestion, I went to Zambia's Eastern Province, where one of his former students, by then an officer of language in education, took me on a six-week tour of eight different schools across the province. At each school, I observed lessons of Language and Literacy in early grades (1–4), providing me with a broad impression of the practices and challenges of public schooling in many parts of Southern Africa. I also got to see the notable differences between schools in urban areas and those in rural areas, visible both in their physical condition and students' performance. Whereas the urban schools generally had well-kept buildings and sufficient libraries, the rural schools looked rundown and often lacked books, furniture and housing for teachers. While the urban students generally spoke loudly and eagerly, both in lessons conducted in English and the local language (Nyanja) prevailing in Eastern Province, students from more remote areas appeared more quiet and reluctant to participate in class. This spurred my interest towards the influence of children's linguistic and demographic backgrounds on their school experiences. During interviews, teachers described the various challenges facing the schooling of rural children, usually associated with a lack of financial, intellectual and emotional support from parents, who often had little schooling themselves. But as insightful as these responses were, they gave me little information on children's and parents' own perceptions of school.

After the tour of schools had ended, I went back to Lusaka and the University of Zambia (UNZA) to plan my remaining fieldwork. One day I got to talk to a student of Language and Education, 27-year-old Khama Hang'ombe, who had recently assisted the agricultural fieldwork of another PhD fellow and was looking for work. Apart from being a proficient speaker and writer of Zambia's seven regional languages, Khama had been trained in sociolinguistic methods and theories, a field he was very passionate about – and I quickly realised he could become a major asset to the study, not only as a translator but also as a qualified researcher and colleague. He told me about the rural community of Hang'ombe in Southern Province, where he had grown up, and how he would spend time with his family there whenever he had the chance to go back. This was unusual among UNZA students, who mostly stayed in Lusaka during weekends to study or spend time with their friends. I was curious about Khama's strong attraction to 'village life', as he called it, and how he planned such a life for himself, irrespective of his high level of education and aspirations of studying abroad. At one point, I suggested that we conduct fieldwork in Hang'ombe Village itself. I realised how this might put Khama in a difficult situation, positioning him both as researcher and informant and evoking issues of loyalty and bias. However, as we continued to meet and discuss these and other aspects of the study, the advantages of collaborating with a locally known, highly qualified research assistant in an environment otherwise difficult for me to access became so obvious that I decided to proceed with Khama's consent. He called his father Benson Hang'ombe, who invited us to come and stay with him and his wife Sarah, his daughter Minivah and her five children between the ages of two months and eleven years, three of whom frequented the local school. Through a series of incidental events, I thus ended up living with a family of three generations in the Tonga community of Hang'ombe for about nine months, providing close access to daily village life. Khama remained my primary research assistant, colleague and interpreter throughout this work, ensuring a continuous stream of discussion, testing and adjustment of questions and methodological procedures. I elaborate further on the advantages and potential drawbacks associated with this close collaboration below.

Constructing the Field

Every morning during my first month in Hang'ombe, Khama and I escorted his three nieces Talala (11), Mududu (9) and Lushomo (8) to Mbabala Basic School in the township, about 3 km from the homestead. At school, we observed and recorded the different lessons of, primarily, the lower grade levels (1–4), followed by interviews with teachers on their work practices and student experiences. Mbabala teachers gave similar replies to the ones in Eastern Province, underlining their difficulties with taking students – especially the 'slow' ones from remote rural areas – through the curriculum. These conversations familiarised me with commonly perceived distinctions between townshippers and villagers, along with significant issues of educational politics, unemployment, poverty, alcoholism, prostitution, teenage pregnancies and HIV / Aids.

In the afternoons, Khama assisted me in the transcription and translation of classroom recordings, which we then analysed through basic sociolinguistic categories. After a few weeks, I became increasingly interested in students' out-of-school lives, and so we began following different children around, recording their interactions on their way home from school, playing in the yard or working with peers or parents in the gardens. Some days we asked a group of children permission to follow and record them wherever they were going, or we asked them to carry the recorder themselves. I elaborate on the collection and processing of these recordings further below, including issues of interpretation. This gradual change of research focus was not only inspired by my increasing involvement in the daily matters of Hang'ombe children and their families but also by a number of critical works on the schooling and socialisation of children, including Shirley Bryce Heath's legendary *Ways with Words* (Heath 1983) on the literacy and language socialisation of children growing up in two 1970s working-class communities in south-eastern United States. I was impressed by her vivid descriptions of relationships and interactions between family members and the rich contextual basis these descriptions provided for her analyses of the children's experiences and trajectories of school.

Pursuing such close linguistic ethnographic descriptions of Hang'ombe children's everyday lives, I decided to focus my observations on the inhabitants of four local homesteads (*minzi*) who had welcomed me during my first month in the village in mid 2008 and included Khama's extended family. Differing in size, socio-economic status and years of schooling, these homesteads together comprised about twenty 6–12-year-old boys and girls, most of whom attended Mbabala Basic School along with a large number of younger and older siblings, cousins, aunts, uncles, parents, grandparents and extended relatives:[1]

The Mweemba munzi comprised four different households, all sustaining themselves and each other through farming and gardening on their relatively large piece of land. 6-year-old Emma, her sister Luyaba (9), their father Roy (32) and mother Estar (27) lived one side of a large house, the girls sharing one room and their parents another. The other half of the house held the girls' paternal uncle Motty (31), his wife Jackie (28) and their four children: 9-year-old Daala, his twin sister Disteria and their brothers Munsanje (7) and Edson (6), along with the children's 9-year-old cousin Richwel (9) and their young aunt Frida (10), four of whom we met in the introduction. Behind this house was a small one-room shelter in which 9-year-old Brian and his brothers Gary (5) and John (3) lived with their mother Irene (33), who had recently divorced and returned to her parents' home from a neighbouring village. The last household held all the children's mutual grandparents, Milo (65) and Mairon (63), along with their 26-year-old nephew Alfred (26), who had stayed with them for the past year to assist them in the fields.

The Hambuulo munzi consisted of 9-year-old Luyando and her three brothers Calleen (7), Oscar (10) and Roy (13), their mother Lila (32) and their father Levias (38), all living in a large house holding expensive furniture and a collection of religious books. As a high school graduate and leader of the local Seventh Day Adventist church council, Levias Hambuulo and his family were highly respected by many villagers. The family also included a 17-year- old daughter, Chipo, who at the time of my stay was finishing secondary school in the neighbouring town of Choma.

The Phiri munzi contained three households divided into four houses: 45-year-old Love and her husband Shadrik (48) lived with their daughters Mwiinga (15), Brenda (9) and Miyoba (7), along with Love's granddaughters Malilwe (11) and Shimbi (6) in one house, while their three sons Julu (11), Solomon (9) and Clever (6) slept together in a separate house next to the main house. Love's 20-year-old nephew Obrian, his wife Sarah (18) and their young baby Junior lived in a small house opposite the main house, while Shadrik's maternal aunt Elizabeth (64) stayed in another small house with her three grandchildren Eden (3), Nchimunya (7) and Banda (10), whose parents had divorced and both lived far away. The Phiris owned relatively little land and relied heavily on the children's collective workforce, especially during the harvest months.

The Hang'ombe munzi – Khama's extended family with whom I stayed for most of my time in Hang'ombe Village – consisted of his sister Minivah (38), who stayed in her own small house, and her five children Lweendo (1), Habeenzu (3), Lushomo (8), Mududu (9) and Talala (11), who slept in the main house with their paternal grandfather Benson (82) and his wife Sarah (67). During my stay in 2008–9, Minivah's nieces Mutinta (13) and Senefa (6) came from Livingstone to stay with the family, since their mother had remarried and could not bring them with her. The family was also joined by Benson's nephew Talis (28), who had gotten into trouble in a neighbouring village and was sent to Benson's home for re-education, along with the children's male cousin Sinyimbwe (20) who lived in a neighbouring homestead and came to visit quite often.

As it was risky for women to walk around between homesteads at night, I often left the recorder with a parent or grandparent, asking him or her to record the family's interactions around the fire at night. These family conversations revealed interesting themes to me, such as the 'goodness of schooling' (*bubotu bwa cikolo*) and the alleged (mis)demeanours of other community members that were often debated enthusiastically around family fires. Along with recordings of children's play, these conversations spurred my curiosity towards adult discourse and its appropriation by school-aged children. Comparing my observations and recordings from the four different Hang'ombe homesteads, I found certain differences, for example, in terms of the social and linguistic leeway allowed to children and the degree of apparent interest in children's schooling. However, as these differences appeared relatively minor compared with the common topical and interactional features appearing across the families, listed above, I have chosen to speak more generally about 'Hang'ombe families' and 'Hang'ombe children', although such categories obviously remain analytical constructs. All names and places have been anonymised, and personal information like ages and social affiliations have in some cases been slightly modified in order to maintain informants' anonymity. The utterings and exchanges depicted throughout the book are all direct quotations, however.

Along with my ongoing talks with Khama, my relationship with his older sister Minivah formed an initiation into life in Hang'ombe Village. Being almost the same age as me and quite proficient in English, Minivah quickly became both an ally and a close friend with whom I had many nightly talks about her life as a woman and single mother of five young children, including her longing to go back to school and pursue her dreams of becoming a nurse, and about her friendships and daily encounters with people in the community. I would reciprocate with my own observations and experiences as a single Western woman placed in a foreign, highly family-oriented society, and we would laugh at the paradoxes entailed in this experience. As I became more and more engaged in the daily life experiences of children, Minivah also became a central source of information on childhood, parenting and schooling. Later on in fieldwork, Minivah interviewed some of her friends on their relationships to their children, and she often joined my discussions with Khama, following the study's evolvement and suggesting new issues for us to pursue. Finally, I conducted many hours of both formal and informal interviews with Khama's 82-year-old father Benson, who as a former headman had an immense knowledge about the community, its history and its members. Through Khama's translation, Benson told me about the forced resettlement of the community in the early twentieth century, following the arrival of white industrial farmers (see Lancaster and Vickery 2007). We discussed the political system of headmanship and the traditions and challenges of maize farming, cattle herding, establishing an honourable home and ensuring both the formal and informal education of one's children. All in all, Khama and his family members came to be significant to both the planning and conduct of my fieldwork, and this study has come to reflect, perhaps more than anything, everyday life unfolding in a close-knit intergenerational household.

Studying Children's Lives

As researchers have increasingly recognised in the past decades, ethnographic studies involving children require an enhanced research ethics protecting the privacy and integrity of the individual child, both in terms of public and personal disclosure (Friedl 2004; Kampmann 2006). Such caution may be particularly urgent in studies based in postcolonial societies – still conducted mainly by Western-based researchers – where the obtainment of children's 'informed consent' to participate in extensive, often quite opaque research projects is problematised not only by a presumed incomprehension of its possible consequences for participants but also by the complex power structures evoked by such research, reproducing and potentially exploiting stereotypical roles of the Western 'subject' and the non-Western 'object'. This also regards the current study. The steep generational hierarchy prevailing across Hang'ombe and the fact that I, as a Western woman and visitor, and Khama, an adult, highly educated man from a well-respected local family, were both ascribed with such high levels of status made it difficult for children – as well as their parents, teachers and other adults – to dismiss our invitations, even though we continued to ask for their consent, carefully explaining our broader research objective and promise of anonymity.

Although I tried toning down my appearance – by wearing casual clothes, joking with both adults and children and eating, sleeping and helping out (almost) on the same terms as other women in the household – I remained utterly foreign to the majority of the people I lived and worked among. When we visited neighbouring households, people would insist on serving me tea and biscuits and giving me their best chair, and when I sometimes suggested that I assist children in their work chores or sit and eat with them on the floor, it was usually politely but firmly denied. Many of the children I spent time with gradually accepted me as a kind of auntie or extended relative, sitting close to me, flicking through my books and pictures with great interest, but I still found it difficult to deduce anything but shy, monosyllabical utterances from them as response to my questions about their doings, interests and concerns, even when assisted by their mothers or older siblings. Such shyness seemed to reflect both a lack of familiarity with me and the fact that questions addressed to children by other adults – whether parents, relatives or teachers – generally served a regulatory purpose, rather than an inquisitive one, and that adults would rarely expect or encourage children below the age of 10–12 to make elaborate, unregulated utterances to adults. On my suggestion, Khama conducted interviews with fifteen different children between the ages of 8–12, who all gave him hesitant replies about their school experiences and future dreams. I also asked a whole class of grade eight students at Mbabala Basic to write about their 'dreams for the future' as part of their English class, eliciting interesting (but brief) perspectives on things such as the relationship between schooling and material wealth. Apart from teaching me about the fear and authority surrounding children's general relationship to adults, however, none of these initiatives gave me much insight into children's own experiences and perspectives.

This experience changed as Khama and I began recording interactions occurring among different school-aged boys and girls while cooking, herding cattle, playing games or helping out their fathers or mothers in the field – particularly when we abstained from observing and allowed children to carry the recorder around themselves. Although we kept asking for children's consent before turning on or handing them the recorder and they were thus aware of its presence, I perceive these recorded interactions as representations of how children might interact and position themselves towards each other and their everyday environments. Obviously, the children's reactions to me and my questions during interviews were just as real, revealing important practices among children and adults, which I have included in my analyses. The issue at stake here is thus not so much one of authenticity but rather the fact that the employment of different methodological means – in this case, interviews vs. the recording of everyday speech – may and mostly will generate different kinds of data, perhaps especially in ethnographic work among young children.

Producing Data

Initially, the children seemed puzzled by this interest in their daily activities and would frequently comment about it in their interactions, discussing how I might listen to their voices and utterances later on. Sometimes they included the recorder as a fictitious person in their play, most likely caused by the similarity between the black, frizzy windbreaker placed on top of the recorder and the hairstyle of a young African child. One example of this is the interaction between Khama's niece Talala (11) and her brother Habeenzu (3) below, recorded one evening in the main house while Talala was ironing the school uniform of her sister Lushomo, who was playing nearby. Khama had left the recorder sitting on a chair right next to the ironing board, and no adults were present during the children's interaction:

1. Talala [to Habeenzu]: Kuti upye, ndakuuma, nsekokuleka.
   If you get burnt, I'll beat you, I won't spare you.

2. Habeenzu [pointing to recorder]: Ino oyu?
   What about this one?

3. Talala: Ni?
   Who?

4. Habeenzu: Oyu uukkede waawa.
   This one [the recorder] sitting here.

5. Talala [jokingly]: Watyani?
   What has he done?

6. Habeenzu: Kuti apye, umuume.
   If he gets burnt, you should beat him.

7. Talala [laughing]: Iiyi, ndamuuma.
   Yes, I'll beat him.

8. Habeenzu [to recorder, jokingly]: Ulapya, kozwa awa.
   You'll get burnt, move away from there.

As appears, the presence of the lit recorder did not necessarily make the children fall silent or leave, even though that did indeed happen at times. Instead, the recorder often became a focus of interaction, in this case evoking children's own playful experiments with parental authority. In the interaction below, 9-year-old Luyaba, her sister Emma (6) and their two visiting cousins Maya (10) and Namwiinga (7) recorded themselves one afternoon while pealing maize outside the kitchen building in the Mweemba homestead. Luyaba solemnly warned her peers how the recorder would 'pick your voices' (*kabweza majwi eenu*), indicating that they should guard their speech in its presence:

1. Luyaba: Olo kalakugambya, kabweza majwi eenu.
   It may surprise you, it [the recorder] is picking your voices.

2. Maya: Inzi?
   What?

3. Emma: Nka lekkoda. Olo waamba kuti 'Ma!' kala lekkoda.

    It's a recorder. Even when you say 'Ma!' it'll record you.

4. Maya [to Namwiinga]: Waamba kuti kalekkoda ...?

    She [Luyaba] said it [the recorder] has recorded ...?

5. Luyaba: Kufwumbwa ncooamba, kala lekkoda. Olo watukana, kalalekkoda.

    Whatever you say, it records. Even you make an insult, it'll record.

Children often seemed to moderate their speech when exposed to the recorder, perceiving it as a kind of surrogate adult. In line with children's reactions to me and my questions, I see such reactions as an integral part of the children's configuration of the world around them, rather than as a methodological or analytical restraint. Especially early on, my enterprise of observing and recording in all sorts of places was the source of great amusement to children and adults alike, and we would sometimes extend this amusement during sessions of collective listening to the day's recordings around the computer at night. After a while, however, the children seemed to familiarise themselves and gradually lose interest in us as we followed them around and recorded them, chatting while walking home from school, taking instructions from parents in the garden or telling stories and jokes around the kitchen fire at night. Other actors would appear in these interactions, like grandparents, uncles, friends and cousins living nearby, and the scope of our recordings gradually evolved, continuously led by children's daily trajectories rather than by a preset plan. If one child or more sat quietly by the fire at night while adults were chatting, I would ask permission to light the recorder. On Saturday mornings, Khama and I followed different children to Sabbath School and recorded their interactions with peers and church elders, and if one of them had to make an errand to the township or a neighbouring homestead, one of us would go along, recording whatever interaction he or she would engage in on the way. Like children, adults were puzzled by our enterprise at first, turning shy or inquiring about what we were doing – but as they came to know me, most people relaxed, especially after realising my genuine interest in their children's schooling.

This compliance from children and adults towards me may partially be ascribed to the relatively modest appearance of my small voice recorder, resembling the simple mobile phones possessed by many adult villagers in 2008–9. Many linguistic ethnographers now use video as a supplement to sound recordings and field observations, recognising the strong significance of bodily gestures, mimics and gaze to human interaction. While I acknowledge the ethnographic value of such visual information, my estimation was that the presence of a video camera might make villagers uncomfortable and affect their social and linguistic conduct – especially children's – to a degree that was inexpedient to the production of data and to my basic relationship with informants. Children and adults frequently carried the recorder in their shirt pockets or aprons, recording themselves while walking, relaxing or working in the fields and households. Such self-recording would have demanded much more effort and meticulousness from actors with a video camera, and although visual recordings might have allowed for more detailed depictions of everyday practices and interactions, I assess that these interactions in many cases might have been less spontaneous and animated than the ones produced through audio.

Between August 2008 and May 2009, Khama and I gradually accumulated a corpus of about 200 'speech recordings' of 1–2 hours each, varying broadly in terms of actors, activities, domains and topics discussed but always involving the presence of one or more 6–12-year-old children. I continued visiting Mbabala Basic School along with a few schools in neighbouring, more remote villages, observing classes and recess activities and interviewing teachers. Every other afternoon, Khama and I sat at the large table in his family's *cikuta* (visitors' hut), going through recordings and discussing findings. Although my chiTonga gradually improved enough for me to identify the character and central foci of the recorded interactions, I remained dependant on Khama's proficiency and sociolinguistic training for the conduct of close linguistic analysis. As we went through recordings, I would ask him to transcribe and translate into English the parts where certain themes or practices appeared, illustrated in Figure 1.1.

Going through these transcriptions and translations several times, we discussed different social and linguistic observations, like children's experiments with adult figures and the solemn moral discourse permeating both children's and adults' talk. These observations also informed my ongoing conversations and interviews with several parents, grandparents, church elders and teachers on children's education, along with more general aspects and concerns of community life. Khama's role as interpreter, 'cultural broker' and sociolinguistic researcher was thus crucial to the processing and early analysis of data, providing me with important social, linguistic and historical information.

Transcriptions/translations October 2008

Recording:	Focus:
270908 Mududu and Lushomo singing outside	– *songs, jokes, comments, topics discussed*
270908 Malilwe and Brenda telling stories at night	– *transcribe all stories, including comments*
280908 Claude writing letter for his father Benson	– *discussing writing, family conflict, father- son*
290908 Daala and Munsanje in the garden with parents	– *informal/'silent' learning, atmosphere, planning*
300908 Child Theatre, New Apostolic Church	– *'moral' learning, church views on local life*
300908 The Mweemba family at night	– *family night talk, stories, jokes, relationships*
011008 Phiri children playing and chatting outside	– *jokes, fights, 'moral talk', topics discussed*
011008 Minivah, Love, Patricia, Talala etc.	– *married/unmarried women talking among children*
021008 Hambuulo family at night	– *children, 'family dynamics', topics discussed, jokes*
041008 Shadrik and Clever ploughing	– *directives, silent learning, intimacy, father-son*
051008 Clever, Solomon and Julu herding cattle	– *'boys talk', distributing chores, topics discussed*
081008 Lushomo and Lweendo + later Sarah	– *child talk to babies, grandmother orders*
081008 Visitors from Lusaka, Livingstone etc.	– *socio-economic differences, power and speech between distant relatives*

Figure 1.1 Example of my directions for Khama's initial transcripts and translations of recordings.

Translating the Field

Originally planning fieldwork in Zambia's Eastern Province, I spent some months in early 2008 acquiring a basic proficiency in the lingua franca chiNyanja, which carries certain lexical, phonetic and grammatical similarities to chiTonga, both being Bantu languages. During my first three months in Hang'ombe, Khama and his sister Minivah took shifts giving me daily language lessons, which along with our ongoing processing of recordings gave me a basic proficiency in colloquial chiTonga. As noted above, however, I relied on Khama's selected transcriptions and translations to conduct close linguistic analyses of the recorded data, which were a central methodological concern to this study. More than other scientists, anthropologists have sought to familiarise themselves with the social customs prevailing in their fields of study, conducting longitudinal fieldwork, living among and seeking to immerse themselves in the lives and concerns of their main informants. This obviously includes people's communicative practices, especially among linguistic anthropologists, who often spend months and years acquiring the language or languages prevailing in their fields of study (e.g. Moore 2009). Fluent language skills remains an ideal anthropological prerequisite for 'learn[ing] the culture and the social system which are conceptualized in the language' (Evans-Pritchard 1951: 79), for 'symboliz[ing] a commitment, a respect and appreciation for the cultural heritage of the people they study' (Duranti 1997: 111) and for basically understanding 'what is going on' in the field (Duranti 1997: 110).

However, this ideal has been increasingly challenged, as increased social and political globalisation have prompted anthropologists to work across social, physical and geographical contexts (Marcus 1995), often entailing multilingual communication practices. The fact that ethnographers' linguistic (in)proficiency has remained a kind of taboo has brought a call for more transparency around issues of translation, including a debate about the building of communicative competence among ethnographers and the employment of local interpreters (Moore 2009). As part of this debate, linguistic anthropologist Axel Borchgrevink lists potential advantages of involving one or more socially and linguistically skilled interpreters in fieldwork, like building confidentiality among informants prior to and during the collection of data, accessing otherwise inaccessible sites and arenas, checking against exaggerations and false information, recalling and discussing earlier fieldwork events and participating as both language teacher and key informant to the ethnographer (Borchgrevink 2003). Such aspects obviously rely on the individual interpreter and his or her communicative skills and relationship to the people and field of study, and potential misinterpretation of data must be forestalled through careful training of both researchers and interpreters and continuous dialogue between them (Borchgrevink 2003: 104–5).

Based on my own fieldwork experience, I assent to the importance of the ethnographer familiarising herself as much as possible with the local social, linguistic and other practices of the people studied, but I see no conflict between such familiarisation and collaborating with a locally known, highly skilled interpreter. When going through recordings, Khama would direct my attention to silences and tones of voice, to personal and generational relationships between actors and to the social and moral decora underlying their interactions, creating the basis for a level of social and cultural contextualisation that would have been difficult for me to obtain on my own, even with greater linguistic proficiency and more time on my hands. I would cross-check many of Khama's suggestions, comparing them with my own observations and going through recordings with Minivah and a few local teachers – and, later on, with my colleagues at the University of Zambia. My recurrent discussions with Khama and a few other, more provisionally employed local interpreters have thus allowed a space of continuous inquiry of great value to the final analyses.

Transcriptions

As noted in the introduction, my analyses of everyday talk among children, their peers and family members focus predominantly on the content of interactions and less on their linguistic formats, although I do examine children's creative appropriations of different discourses and authoritative registers available to them, like 'parent talk', 'teacher talk', and 'preacher talk', especially in Chapters 3 and 4. In the attempt to make the data easily accessible to non-linguist readers, I adopt what linguistic anthropologist Mary Bucholtz has called a naturalised transcription – that is, 'one in which the process of transcription is made less visible through *literacization*, the privileging of written over oral features' (Bucholtz 2000: 1461). The transcripts thus follow general orthographic standards of chiTonga and English, while the use of English or 'English-like' words and expressions in chiTonga-dominated speech has been marked with bold. Instead of marking extraverbal traits like intonation, pitch and the length of pauses and sounds with symbols as in conventional linguistic analyses, I have sought to depict speakers' extraverbal communication through interpretive descriptions placed in hard brackets, like [jokingly], [sternly], [solemnly], [in low voice] etc. Although Khama and I would sometimes replay recordings to participants and ask them to comment on recorded extracts, most of these descriptions reflect our own subjective interpretations of speakers' stances and attitudes in specific instants of interaction. Such interpretations of speakers' shifting attitudes should obviously be subject to critical reflection from readers, like all qualitative analysis. However, as Bucholtz notes, any transcriptive method reflects a bias towards speakers and their speech practices (Bucholtz 2000: 1461). As noted earlier, I have aimed to make the displayed data extracts as accessible to readers as possible while trying to maintain verbal accuracy and detail.

Conclusion

The course of research for this book has been marked by a series of topical and methodological shifts as my fieldwork evolved and new questions and possibilities emerged. From an initial focus on mother tongue education, I ended up analysing social matters of childhood, family and village life through the lens of children's everyday talk. This included classroom observations and teacher interviews, but the ethnographic data sustaining my analyses most powerfully were conducted in homes, fields and gardens, far away from the official domains of school. Unlike the assumptions of many educational stakeholders, the school may not always form the privileged locus of children's learning and social development. In a community concerned with the maintenance of basic physical and social security and where the school's practices and orientations remain somewhat remote, children's early education may be informed by several, sometimes conflicting rationales. Exploring such rationales and including less obvious learning practices and arenas in the study of children's schooling – like their kin and sibling interactions while working or their eavesdropping on adults' talk at night – may extend our understanding of educational challenges in the majority world and give insights into children's linguistic repertoires and competences that are rarely acknowledged by educational stakeholders. As anthropological students and researchers will know, topical and methodological shifts are relatively common in longitudinal ethnographic studies, especially early on when the researcher is less established in her theoretical and regional field of study. Numerous and constant choices have to be made in the field – often based on quick estimations – and elements of chance and intuition may determine our analytical outcomes more than we like to admit. In my case, meeting my future research assistant Khama Hang'ombe in the late spring of 2008 after six weeks of unsatisfying school visits in eastern Zambia and being invited to stay in his family's home for the following nine months was an element of chance that I could not possibly have predicted when preparing my study. The choice to abandon my previous plan, accept this invitation and enrol Khama and his family extensively in the research process happened in the course of a few days and was based partly on a growing desperation – fearing that I might thwart my entire fieldwork and produce only shallow analyses if I kept my preliminary plan – and partly on intuition and curiosity, sensing a unique opportunity to move much closer to the people and tangible concerns involved in the field I was trying to study. Embracing the potential benefits of such precariousness in the research process – e.g. by enhancing students and researchers' institutional latitude for spending time trying out different approaches in the field – might entail more 'messy' and unlinear studies, but it might also uncover valuable questions and insights that would otherwise remain concealed.

Note

1 .See Figure 0.1. All personal and family names have been changed for the anonymity and protection of informants.

🌿 2

'KNOW A DEAD MAN'S FEET BY HIS CHILD'
Family Life in a Changing Society

> As parents, we try to teach our children to be good people in society. If you are not a good person, if you don't care about others or cooperate with people, nobody will like you. And so even if you are in deep trouble, they will not come to help you.
>
> —Irene, 33-year-old mother of three

> No one has to tell a friend, 'You have to work while the rains are still on.' Everyone knows that you have to work and finish everything while the rains are still on.
>
> —Noah, 74-year-old senior headman, father and grandfather of 14 children

One Wednesday afternoon in early December 2008, 9-year-old Mududu was sitting by the kitchen fire, cooking *nsima* or maize porridge for her family's evening meal in the Hang'ombe homestead. Seated next to her was her mother Minivah (38), closely observing Mududu's actions, her 3-year-old brother Habeenzu and her baby sister Lweendo, who alternated between Minivah and Mududu's laps. The nsima was usually prepared by Mududu's older sister Talala (11), but she was busy that day escorting her grandmother to visit a diseased cousin in a neighbouring village. Having assisted her mother and older sister in the kitchen numerous times, Mududu managed the cooking largely on her own, mixing cornmeal and water while constantly stirring the big iron pot. At one point, Mududu accidentally pushed over a small water pot:[1]

1. Minivah [to Mududu, annoyed]: Iih! Watila, watila meenda. Kabweze [kapika].

   > *Iih! You have poured, you have poured down the water. Pick it up [the small pot].*

   [Mududu picks up the pot.]

2. Habeenzu [quietly, mimicking Minivah]: Atika meenda atika, atika meenda, atika meenda atika, atika meenda atika…

   > *You have poured down the water, you have poured it down. You have poured water down, you have poured water down, water down …*

3. Minivah [to Mududu]: Gusya nkuni eyo amulilo, ilaunsya mpoto. [To Lweendo] Babyyy! …

   > *Remove that firewood from the fire, it will make the pot fall. [To Lweendo] Babyyy! …*

   [Mududu removes the firewood from the fire and returns to stirring the nsima.]

4. Habeenzu [mimicking Minivah]: Babyyy … [To Minivah] Mwana unyonka tunwe.

   > *Babyyy … [To Minivah] The baby is sucking [her] fingers.*

5. Minivah [to Mududu]: Eyo nkuni amwiibikke kabotu.

   > *That firewood should be put properly.*

   [Minivah hands Lweendo to Mududu and adjusts the log under the pot.]

6. Minivah [to Mududu]: Leta mwana kutegwa ubikke kabotu ncili. Bikka kabotu ncili.

   > *Hand [me] the baby so you can put the grinder properly. Put the grinder properly.*

   [Mududu hands the baby back to Minivah and adjusts the grinder.]

7. Mududu [strict, to Habeenzu]: Habeenzu, sowa lingo elyo!

   > *Habeenzu, throw that mango away!*

   [Habeenzu takes the mango and throws it outside the kitchen house.]

8. Habeenzu [from outside]: Ndalisowa lino

   > *I have thrown it away now.*

   [Minivah calls Habeenzu from inside the kitchen.]

9. Minivah [to Habeenzu, impatiently]: Koya ukalete knife kuli Shimbi. Habeenzu, koya ukalete knife kuli Shimbi.

> *Go and get the knife from Shimbi. Habeenzu, go and bring the knife from Shimbi!*

10. Minivah [to Mududu]: Ubambe rice tujike.

> *Prepare the rice so that we can cook it.*

[Mududu starts sorting and washing the rice. Occasionally, she stirs the nsima.]

11. Habeenzu [outside]: Tatujisi swebo?

> *Don't we have one [a knife]?*

12. Minivah: Ey?

> *What?*

13. Habeenzu: Tatujisi swebo?

> *Don't we have one?*

14. Minivah [annoyed]: Baya bantu babweza yesu. Fwambaana!

> *Those people have taken ours. Get going!*

As appears, Mududu quietly obeys her mother's instructions, picking up the pot, adjusting the firewood, stirring the nsima and preparing the rice (lines 1, 3, 5, 10). In accordance with local customs, an adolescent girl like 9-year-old Mududu must possess basic practices of cooking and housekeeping, and the degree of diligence with which she performs these chores is likely to be scrutinised and evaluated, not only by her mother but also by her siblings, relatives and bypassing neighbours. Among all the Hang'ombe families I visited, girls' and young women's housework was subject to ongoing judgement and regulation from fellow family members and visitors, associating a young woman's housekeeping skills with her basic moral and eventual eligibility for marriage. In comparison, 3-year-old Habeenzu's playful twaddle is largely ignored by his mother and sister above, except when ordering him to throw away a mango (line 7) and to bring a knife from the neighbouring house of Minivah's niece Shimbi (line 9, 14). Mududu here assumes the role of assisting monitor of her younger brother (line 7), a role increasingly expected of her as she grows up.

In this chapter, I pursue the routines and relationships framing children's early lives in Hang'ombe Village, centring on their participation in basic household chores and their interactions with different family members. Like in many parts of rural Africa, most

Hang'ombe children were born into close family networks, and the village was predominated by 8–10 large intermarried families, making practically all villagers related through marriage or kin. People mostly referred to family by the term *mukwasyi*, covering one's father, mother or mothers, siblings and other relatives living in one's homestead, along with one's immediate matrilineal kin – mother's parents, sisters and brothers, and their daughters and sons. In polygynous marriages, which were found in about 35% of households and were on the rise among younger men and women in 2008, children were expected to address both their biological mother and her co-wife or -wives by the respectful *baama* (mother), although most differed between their own and their classificatory mothers in terms of intimacy and support. Associating closely with their matrilineal relatives, children also addressed their mother's siblings as *baama* (mother) and *batata* (father), who, even if living far away, were expected to provide for the children's needs through their formative years, paying school fees, bringing clothes and gifts and perhaps taking them into their homestead by the loss of one or both biological parents. Likewise, children were expected to assist their maternal relatives living nearby, with girls helping out in the garden, household and nursing of children and boys joining the farming and, eventually, making financial subsidies or taking care of relatives in their own home. For most members, the concept of family or *mukwasyi* thus included a large number of people, covering both their maternal relatives living in neighbouring homesteads or further away and the paternal relatives living in their physical home. The fertility rate was high, and many homesteads held 5–10 children below the age of twelve. In daily life, the homestead or *munzi* was centre of social interaction and concern in young children's lives, and in spite of its ongoing fluctuation, it was the most important arena for framing children's early socialisation. A typical homestead consisted of a number of clay houses, a kitchen house and perhaps a separate, open house for visitors and nightly gatherings (*cikuta*), all circled around a large courtyard, often with a large bougainvillea at the centre. Married women mostly possessed a house of their own in their husband's homestead, and children usually slept together with their biological mother until the age of five or six, after which they might move to a separate house for boys and girls respectively. While men and boys above the age of fifteen generally ate in the cikuta, children would eat with their mother and female relatives in the kitchen house.

While members generally strove towards the preservation and unity of family bonds, the composition of homesteads often changed.

Grown daughters left their parental home when marrying, perhaps leaving their children of previous engagements behind, and returned for varying periods of time with more children if divorcing. Ageing parents and grandparents moved to their sons' homes, and young grandchildren, cousins, nieces and nephews might be adopted as 'dependent' household assistance by more prosperous relatives. Fathers and adolescents sometimes relocated for schooling or employment in urban centres, and a child might not see her siblings or biological parents, especially her father, for months or years, as long distances and expensive transport were solid obstacles for most families. Unstable harvest results and opportunities for paid employment formed severe predicaments, and although several members shared stories of relatives or acquaintances who had been financially successful doing business in Lusaka or other urban centres in the region, most adults expressed an experience of their general living conditions and possibilities for themselves and their children having worsened in the past few decades.

In the face of such precarity, people manoeuvred in a tight moral economy of reciprocity and interdependence. Children and adolescents relied on parents, grandparents, older siblings, aunts and uncles for their general nurture and school-related expenses, the latter increasing drastically if they proceeded with schooling after grade seven. A young woman wanting to marry needed financial and psychological support from both her parents and her future in-laws, especially if they adhered to the traditional payment of *lobola* or bride price. If a young man sought to cultivate his own garden or field and extend his own population of cattle – both vital to his options for marriage, especially if he did not pursue further education and/or formal employment – he often relied on the wealth and goodwill of close and extended family members, yielding him a life-long debt to his benefactors. Parents relied on the labour and support of their children, especially as parents themselves grew older and less able-bodied. A father and husband might need the periodical support of neighbours and extended relatives, lending him a plough or helping him with the thatching of a new roof. A mother and wife relied on the extensive support system of fellow women, keeping her informed on community matters and assisting her with the nurture and upbringing of her children and with the conduct of household and garden work during periods of illness, etc. And a senior man might fall sick during the harvesting season and perhaps require his wife or daughters to plead with their neighbours for help with the ploughing or nurturing of land, and recurrent household undertakings like building a house or thatching a roof might involve the assistance of nearby relatives, especially if no or few adult men were present in the home. Like many small communities across the majority world, Hang'ombe thus formed a meticulous matrix of interdependent relations, manifesting in a widespread, scrupulous concern with the doings of others and the maintenance and sanctioning of moral norms. Transgressing such norms – e.g. by drinking or stealing from family members – posed an obvious and significant threat to the entire extended family, putting both their reputation and basic security at risk. Marketplace talk thus often centred on the actions and concerns of neighbours and relatives, often measured against strict moral parameters. Examples of 'bad behaviour' (*kubula ciimo*) were frequently discussed around family fires at night, mostly including several children eavesdropping quietly on the adults' talk. Cases of theft, mendacity, idleness, substance abuse, witchcraft and sexual looseness were called out and discussed and buttressed by vivid tales of the alleged (mis)conduct of fellow family and community members.

In the pursuit of social stability, most families maintained a relatively steep hierarchy between parents and children, expecting children to remain submissive and alert in the company of adults. This hierarchy was continuously maintained among the families I studied, revealing its deep social significance along with its apparent need for ongoing consolidation. Parents reminded children that 'You must obey your father' or 'As a grown girl, you must do your chores', just as older children sanctioned their authority over younger peers, who in return sought to advance their position through threats, alignments, jokes or clever remarks. Privacy was a scarce resource and required great discretion, also from children, who were expected to move silently through complex adult lifeworlds from an early age. Within earshot of elders and visitors, children should abstain from boasting, insulting or otherwise using 'bad language' (*mulaka mubi*), and they should adjust their selection of words, tone and topic of speech in accordance with the person(s) they interacted with, acknowledging his or her age, gender, family role and the circumstances under which the interaction took place. They should obey older members' orders, performing household and farming chores with the proper diligence and precision; and, especially as they grew older, they should detect and initiate relevant household tasks on their own, like the weeding of a particular patch in the garden or the preparation of nsima at a particular time in the afternoon, complying with the needs of family members prior to their own. Both boys and girls had to learn to dress properly and keep themselves clean and presentable, especially when leaving the grounds of the homestead. Children's physical and social responsibilities might differ in scale and scope across homesteads, but common to all families was the urgency of acting responsibly and respectably, always identifying and adhering to others' needs and expectations. Each person obviously had interests and schemes of his or her own: gaining better living conditions and financial security for oneself and one's children, ensuring a high status among fellow members (e.g. through dress, prosperity and competence of English) and obtaining personal influence and power through formal education and the holding of prestigious positions in churches, unions, the headmanship etc. But people were constantly reminded of the judgements, needs and expectations of their neighbours and relatives, and they had few ways of hiding inconvenient information from others. Children thus navigated within an omniscient network of supportive and surveilling social relations, trying to meet both their personal needs and other members' demands. This need to accommodate one's personal needs with the wider collective shaped basic ideologies of childrearing and parenting across Hang'ombe families, which I elaborate below.

The Way of Observation

The ownership and overall responsibility of a child were usually ascribed to his or her biological parents, reflected in the honourable custom of naming a mother and father after their first-born child, like *Bina Talala* ('Talala's mother') and *Bausyi Disteria* ('Disteria's father'). In the case of a particularly mischievous child, local judgement mostly fell on the parents, apparent in common proverbs like 'A disobedient child insults the mother' (*Mwana uutanvwi utukanya nyina*) and 'Know a dead man's feet by his child' (*Matende aamufwu azyibilwa kumwana*). Younger women and those with higher school levels tended to be less rigorous than less educated women in their 30s and 40s, but most parents maintained both verbal and physical discipline towards children. Parents' responsibilities were divided by gender, with mothers monitoring the work chores of girls – e.g. collecting firework, sweeping the courtyard, fetching water, nursing their younger siblings and assisting their mothers and other women in the cooking and garden work – and fathers (and occasionally grandfathers) taking boys into the fields to observe their herding of goats and cattle and teach them to lead the oxen in front of the plough. Girls had to acquire all the basic qualities of a well-respected mother and wife in the community, which apart from maintaining the homestead and garden centred on moral traits like diligence, virtue, humility and obedience. Whether or not they succeed in school or business, boys should become skilled farmers before reaching adulthood, weeding the maize plants and operating the plough by themselves. Many young men were given a piece of land around the age of fifteen, acknowledging their status as full-grown farmers and men, ready for the provision of their own family. Ideals of marriage, parenthood and self-sustenance through farming and cattle herding thus permeated parenting practices and ideals across households. Like in other parts of rural Africa, a child's maturity level was assessed by their social competences rather than their biological age (Nsamenang 1992: 143). As children grew more socially responsible, they transcended the category of *bana* (child) to *mukubusyi* (a person growing up) and finally to *muntu uukkwene* (a proper person). Unless when rebuking them, however, adults rarely sat down and explained to children about such ideas. Motty, a 31-year-old father and caretaker of six younger children, explained this practice to me one day while he and I were sitting in the cikuta of his homestead, talking about children and family life:

> We never sit down [and talk to children] the way we are sitting down right now. What we do is different kinds of work, and then children observe what is being done. It is mostly observation. But through our way of life, children will know how to respect elders, how to cook, how to conduct themselves when there are people, visitors and the like – the Tonga way of life. If the children make mistakes or behave wrongly, we tell them that 'this thing is wrong, you should never do this. The right thing is this and this'. So if they abide by that, they are perfect. That is the way of observation. Mostly, children will just observe. They will know that 'this is appropriate and that is not appropriate'.

In her language socialisation study of montagnard children and their families in rural northwestern Cameroon in the early 1990s, Leslie Moore observed a similar approach to children's acquisition of basic chores and principles, including language practices (Moore 1999). In spite of the complex linguistic repertoire employed by adults in this region, including French, a regional language and several local languages (montagnards were generally expected to marry exogamously – that is, outside their ethnic and linguistic group, and women were expected to learn and use their husband's language), parents made few deliberate efforts to enhance children's language skills. Rather than adjust and simplify their speech or 'unravel' the 'unintelligible utterances by a child', as is common in Western middle-class families (Duranti and Ochs 1986, cited in Moore 1999: 337), montagnard parents expected children to learn everyday speech by listening and watching. Moore observed how '[montagnard] children speak far more with peers and sibling caregivers than with adults, and there is little pressure for the child to perform linguistically before she does so spontaneously' (Moore 1999: 337). In Hang'ombe, adults' language repertoires generally seemed slightly less complex than among the montagnards, as they mostly married other Tongas, and chiTonga – one of Zambia's seven regional languages – was applicable to a wide range of local and regional contexts. However, many people still had a relatively advanced command of other regional languages, like chiLozi, chiBemba and chiNyanja, due to media exposure, temporary migration or – increasingly – working in ethnically and linguistically mixed groups of construction workers in the township nearby. Most Hang'ombe adults also had some proficiency in English, and so multilingualism was the norm – as in most other parts of Africa (Whiteley 2018) – rather than the exception. Like among the montagnards, Hang'ombe children were expected to develop appropriate language skills through listening and observing, and they generally interacted far more with their peers and siblings than with adults, including parents.

In daily endeavours, parents thus usually spoke little to children, except for occasional directives, like 'hold [on] like this' (*jata boobu*), 'do it carefully' (*cita kabotu-kabotu*), 'move faster' (*kweendesya*) or 'get going' (*fwambaana*), perhaps accompanied by gestures. Children's work was rarely praised, and I hardly ever observed a school-aged child seek approval from adults. Instead, children's confidence was built through their participation in adults' chores and perhaps an acknowledging glance or intimate tone of voice. An example of this was an exchange occurring between 6-year-old Clever and his father Shadrik while the two of them ploughed the Phiri family's maize field together one January morning in 2009. While Shadrik held the harness and whip, Clever walked beside him with an eye out for bent or broken crops. Making the oxen move steadily while keeping the plough in line was challenging and demanded full concentration. Assisting his father's driving, Clever's job was to control the oxen by shouting their names, Engine and London, and keep them from stepping on bent maize:

1. Shadrik [in stern voice]: Caila.
     Drive the oxen.

2. Clever [to the oxen]: Engine!
     Engine!

3. Shadrik [to the oxen]: Tiye, London.
     Let's go, London.

4. Clever: London!
   London!

5. Shadrik [to the oxen]: Atubeleke.
   Let's work.

6. Clever: Engine!
   Engine!

7. Shadrik: London!
   London!

8. Clever [to the oxen]: Fwolo line.
   Stay in line.

9. Shadrik [to Clever, sternly]: Shaila. Koti, 'Tiya!'
   Keep [the oxen] going. Say 'Let's go!'

10. Clever: Tiya!
    Let's go!

11. Shadrik [to Clever]: Lyakalyatwa ng'ombe
    This maize plant was destroyed by the oxen.

12. Clever: Engine.
    Engine.

13. Shadrik: Fwolo, London … Katubeleka … [To Clever] Kocaila mani.
    Move in line, London … Let's work … [To Clever] You keep driving the oxen.

14. Clever [to the oxen]: Tiya!
    Let's go!

15. Shadrik [to the oxen]: Fwolo!
    Walk in line!

16. Clever [to the oxen]: Fwolo, yebo!
    Walk in line, you!

17. Shadrik [to Clever]: Liimikizye popwe elyo. Liimikizye aleelyo.
    Make that maize plant stand straight. Make that one straight, too.

18. Shadrik [to Clever, mildly]: Maama, kuli mabwe.
    My dear, there are [many] rocks [in the ground].[2]

As appears, a father might speak in stern and concise orders to his son, particularly during demanding work activities like the above (lines 1, 9, 13). Apart from imitating his father's calls, Clever remains quiet – like Mududu towards her mother at the outset of this chapter – carefully following his father's instructions of straightening the maize and driving the oxen. By the end of the extract above, Shadrik assumes a milder tone of voice, telling Clever 'Maama, there are [many] rocks' (line 18). Maama literally meant mother but was also used to express parents' affection towards a young daughter or son. The activity of ploughing allowed Shadrik to continuously assess and promote Clever's performance. Most families relied heavily on children's contributions in gardens, fields and households, and their involvement in adult work chores was aimed first and foremost at increased production levels rather than their personal acquisition of skills. But as social psychologist Barbara Rogoff has described, these two aims are often integrated in societies where children take active part in the daily chores of parents and older siblings from an early age – a practice she and her psychologist and anthropologist colleagues have referred to as *intent participation*:

> In communities in which young children are involved in the mature activities of their family and community, it maybe superfluous for adults to organize lessons and specialized conversations to prepare young children with the skills of schooling, to prepare them for the 'real' world. Instead of doing exercises out of the context of the productive use of skills and information, young children's integration in family and community activities allows them to become increasingly deeply involved through their intent participation. (Rogoff et al. 2003: 183)

More recently, Rogoff has extended her concept of such participatory involvement to *learning by observing and pitching in to family and community endeavours* (Rogoff 2014), emphasising children's role as active contributors to the chores of their family and community members in many rural majority societies. Compared to conventional schooling, this practice offers children an experience of purpose and co-responsibility within their immediate social environments from a very early age. Among Hang'ombe families, children like 9-year-old Mududu and 6-year-old Clever might appear quiet and somewhat subdued while executing their respective parents' commands in shared work chores like cooking and ploughing, but they both display a high level of focus and self-sufficiency, balancing complex demands of diligence, strength and precision without much assistance. As I show further on, Hang'ombe children revealed plenty of verbal agency in the absence of parents and other adults, evaluating each other's work performances and negotiating the social conventions presented to them with their siblings and peers.

In line with Rogoff, evolutionary anthropologists Sara Harkness and Charles Super have demonstrated how parents' and other adults' organisation of children's learning trajectories are deeply embedded in local cultural belief systems. They argue how specific *parental ethnotheories* on child development, family and parenthood affect parents' overt or covert organisation of their children's everyday activities, inducing their development not only of tangible skills but also of the wider social and moral qualities appreciated in local society (Harkness and Super 1992; Harkness et al. 2010). This concurs with my observations of Hang'ombe children's participation in shared household and farming chores, through which parents sought to direct them towards traditional, relatively unequivocal social and moral ideals. Central among these were *kunvwa* ('obedience'), comprising moral qualities of humility, diligence and social responsibility, and *maanu* ('intelligence'), involving wisdom, independence, initiative and perseverance. These concepts both concur with what social psychologists call *socioaffective competence* – an ability to adapt and interrelate with other people promoted in much of rural Africa (Serpell 1993; Super and Harkness 2008). 33-year-old Irene described kunvwa to me this way:

> If, for example, you tell a child 'you must be cooking supper at 18 hours' and then the child cooks at 19 hours instead, it means this child doesn't listen. But if you have told the child to cook at 18 hours, and the child does this exactly, it means this child is able to listen, that he or she has *ulanvwa*.

Though social abilities were perceived as inborn, parents – especially mothers – were held responsible for children's social conduct, and having one's child described as *ulanvwa* ('being obedient') or *ulanvwa kulaigwa* ('abiding by what is told') was an important acknowledgment. Many parental directives were thus aimed at evoking and refining children's *ulanvwa*, especially during work activities. Such treasuring of obedience did not preclude an appreciation of personal initiative, indicated by the concept of *maanu*, which was broadly seen as decisive for a person's material and existential success in life. A highly educated person could be praised as *ula maanu* – having obtained knowledge and success primarily through their own perseverance. Thirty-eight-year-old Minivah Hang'ombe explained the concept this way:

> If a child does something which is needed, something which he or she hasn't been asked to do, like going to the garden and planting something

there, it means that this child has maanu. My children sometimes go to the garden and work without being told. Sometimes they get maize and come and ground it here by themselves, even if I haven't told them. That is maanu … If someone is lazy, they usually don't have maanu, because they won't be doing things correctly. But if someone is strong and works hard, they usually have maanu. They will be full of initiative and do a lot of things.'

Balancing children's development of the qualities of kunvwa and maanu – adaptability and initiative – were crucial for sustaining families in a closely interdependent society, and being 'self-reliant' (*kuzwidilila*) – that is, independent of others' assistance – was seen as inherent to children's maturation. Such ideals are apparent in the extract below, recorded one afternoon in December 2008, when 31-year-old Motty had brought two of his sons, 9-year-old Daala and 6-year-old Edson, to the family's field to help him weed maize to make it receptive to water. As we enter the interaction, the three of them had been working in the garden for a while, using hoes to remove the lower leaves and plants growing too closely. Motty walked slowly beside Daala and Edson, allowing them to observe his actions while monitoring their performance:

1. Motty [to both boys]: Kojwa bbondwe.
   Pluck the weed.

2. Motty [to Edson]: Kocita so. Amumbali kojwa.
   Do like this [showing him how to heap the weeds]. Do it all around [the plant].

3. Motty [to Edson]: Edson, wajwa aya, kosowa kumbali. Daala, ayebo kojwa ku side Oko … Ya, kabotu-kabotu.
   Edson, you should heap the weed together. Daala, pluck the weed on that side … Yes, carefully.

4. Motty [to Daala]: Daala, akakakayuma aka ka Cabbage. Kocita kabotu … Ezyi mpakatwa kamugusya ezyi.
   Daala, this cabbage plant dried up. Do it [the weeding] properly … Pluck one plant if you find two that are too close to each other.

5. Daala [to Edson]: Makwela vwu nkwaagusya, taakwe ncito.
   Remove the leaves that are so low they touch the soil; they are of no use.

6. Motty [to Edson]: Taakwe ncito. Amwaagusye. Oonse aya akaba purple, amwaagusye. [To Daala] Wamana, muboole a side awa.

> *They are of no use. Remove them. All these that have turned purple. Pluck them.*
>
> [To Daala] *When you finish [weeding], you should come to this side.*

7. Daala: Kuno? Ino kuya?

> *Here? Why not over there?*

8. Motty: Okay.

> *Okay.*

9. Daala [to Edson]: Mafwumba aampongo aya. Elyo naakabikkwa.

> *This is goat dung. We applied it to the vegetables a long time ago.*

10. Motty [to Daala]: Mwaamba nzi?

> *What are you talking about?*

11. Daala: Mafwumba aampongo.

> *Goat dung.*

12. Motty: Kayi taamani ayo. Amwaka uuboola anooliko.

> *It lasts long. It will be there up to next year.*

13. Edson [surprised]: Ha! Taamani ino ani.

> *Ha! [I didn't know that] it lasts long.*

14. Motty: Ayo next year anooliko. Next year omu twaakulima …

> *It will be there even next year. When we plant next year.*

15. Edson [to Motty]: Ndilili nitwakausyide mwanja oyu?

> *When did we last dig this cassava?*

16. Motty: Kuzwa leliya nitwausyide. Uyandika kusya.

> *Since that time when we dug it. It needs to be dug.*

17. Edson: Sunu?

> *Today?*

18. Motty: Peepe, kutali sunu.

> *No, not today.*

As appears, parents' directives to children sometimes took the form of more elaborate explanations if activities allowed for it, like weeding maize above. Motty takes time to observe and comment on his sons' performances, telling them to work carefully (*kabotu-kabotu*, line 3) by picking out certain leaves and ensuring enough space between the maize plants so that they do not dry up (line 4). He explains the long-term benefits of applying goat dung to the vegetables, serving as fertiliser 'up to next year' (line 14). 9-year-old Daala has already gained proficiency in most farming chores, like weeding, manuring, ploughing and harvesting, and Motty merely has to remind him of working 'properly' (line 4), directing him to particular patches of the garden (line 8). Daala assists his father in guiding his younger brother Edson, telling him how to remove the lower, purple leaves (line 5) and informing him about goat dung (line 10). Although they mostly remain implicit, Daala and Edson are thus familiarised with the basic qualities of kunvwa and maanu – that is, obedience and attention to the knowledge of elders, along with the tangible benefits of working diligently and with a view to the long term, making their own judgements of crops, plants and soil.

Negotiable Hierarchies

Children, however, would not always follow orders as abjectly as it might appear in the extracts above. Many parents struggled to maintain authority, balancing traditional social values and hierarchies with more modern, individualist ideas that children were exposed to primarily at school, on TV and in the local township. As a contrast to kunvwa and maanu, the term *bunkanwe* ('rude' or 'gossipy') was often applied to children – mostly girls – whose moral education was considered to have failed. Literally, bunkanwe denoted a person's 'mad mouth' – that is, a tendency to quarrel, slander or curse. Most people found it fairly easy to identify a gossipy child as explained by Jackie (28), mother and caretaker of six children, including Daala and Edson above:

> People will know that 'this is a gossipy child' and 'this one is not' from the way a child speaks. It can be a rude way of giving answers. For instance, if an elderly person asks a child 'Where is your mother?' and the child answers that his or her mother has gone to the garden. Then you ask 'What has she gone to do in the garden?' and the child answers rudely by saying 'Don't you know what goes on in the garden?' Then you will know that this child is gossipy.

Emphasising the moral significance of a person's speech, having a 'mad mouth' was linked with defiance, laziness and a general lack of moral. People claimed that children, women and men could be named bunkanwe, but I mostly heard it used to denote young women or girls, in particular their alleged sexual looseness. This connection was also visible in common proverbs like 'That woman is not good for marriage, she is gossipy' (*Uya mukaintu takwatiki, munkanwe*) and 'Better marry a lazy woman than a woman with a [bad] mouth' (*Kona kwata mukaintu mutolo kwiinda sikumulomo*). Like maanu and kunvwa, bunkanwe was regarded an inborn, personal trait that must be curbed through the regulation and positive influence of older family members – and whole families could be denoted as rude or gossipy, explaining a child's misbehaviour by the low moral standards prevailing in their home. Many parents thus worried about the social repercussions of a child disobeying parents or neglecting their chores. As an example of such precaution, the extract below depicts an argument about the washing of dishes between 9-year-old Luyando and her mother Lila (32) in the kitchen of the Hambuulo homestead one evening in January 2009, recorded by the women themselves. The head of this family, 38-year-old Levias Hambuulo, was a well-respected high school graduate and council leader at the local Seventh Day Adventist Church, and both Levias and his wife were known as strong advocates of formal education, striving to support their 17-year-old daughter Chipo's secondary schooling in a neighbouring town. Such appreciation of schooling for both boys and girls did not stop the family from observing more traditional gender roles, however, as appears from the interaction between Luyando and Lila below. At the time of recording, Luyando was sitting by the fire next to Lila, who was preparing nsima for the next day. Luyando's brothers, Calleen (7), Oscar (10) and Roy (13), were sitting outside, relaxing after dinner, while her father Levias was away for a church meeting. At one point, Lila told Luyando to help out with the kitchen work. Rather than complying silently as would usually be expected of her, Luyando insistently tried to dismiss her mother's request:

1. Lila [to Luyando]: Mama, leta cibbo tubone tuzubilile niini.
   Mama, prepare the bowl so that we can start cooking.

2. Luyando: Amubaite bene Calleen basanzye cibbo.
   Call Calleen and the others to wash the bowl.

3. Lila: Baitwe batyani?
   What should they do?

4. Luyando: Basanzye cibbo. Abalo kabanga babeleka.

   They should wash the bowl. They should also work.

5. Lila: Yebo!

   You!

5. Luyando: Ino me, nhu nhu. Sunu, ndakatala.

   Me, no no. Today I'm too tired.

7. Lila: Wakatala kutyani, Mama?

   You are too tired to do what, Mama?

8. Luyando: Kusanzya cibbo.

   To wash the bowl.

9. Lila [sighing]: Ma! Ukatale. Walikusanzya zyiindi zyongaye? Leta muungo kuno. Wamana ulete meenda.

   My! You are tired. How many times did you wash the bowl? Bring the cooking stick. After that you bring water.

10. Luyando [wailing]: Me baama, mebo lino …

    Me mother, me now [not me] …

11. Lila [annoyed]: Iiyi, kutegwa tuzubilile. Hii utume basankwa, mbali ino bayanda kuleta? Naawakabaanzi ncoli so.

    Yes, [go get water] so we can cook. You want the boys to do this, even though you, a girl, is here? I don't know why you're like that.

12. Luyando: Lyoonse, a jilo.

    Always, even yesterday [I had to do most of the work].

13. Lila: Omusimbi basankwa kabasanzya nkoli.

    You, a girl, think that boys should wash when you're there.

14. Luyando: Mpoonya lino kamubalekelezya balo kabaumwine?

    Then you let them stay without doing anything?

15. Lila: Ede cibbo oyu wali kulida wacisanzya, nduwe oocisanzya?

    The one [boy] who was eating from the bowl washed it after eating. Are you the one who washed it?

16. Luyando: Ede ambebo mitiba ndasanzya. Oscar mwamwaambila kuti apyaange alubuwa, kwiina anaapyaanga. Me ndapyaanga.

    I washed the plates. You told Oscar to sweep the yard, but he didn't do it. I swept.

17. Lila: Waamba kuti eyi taili ncito yako. Walo lino uya kukutuswiilizya mboambaula Nana. Uyootuswiilila. Aka kalalemba boonse mbotwaambaula so, aka ncokakkede awa.

> *You said that it wasn't your duty. Nana will hear what we are discussing. She will listen to us. This [recorder] is recording right now, this is why it is here.*

[Lila and Luyando both remain quiet for a while after this. Luyando eventually washes the bowl.]

As noted, Hang'ombe mothers in their twenties and early thirties often displayed a larger leeway towards their school-aged children than older women, negotiating with them rather than giving them an immediate beating or rebuke. When Luyando rejects her mother's request (lines 1, 2), suggesting that her older brothers 'should wash the bowl' (lines 2, 4), since she is 'too tired' to do it herself (lines 6, 8), Lila thus refrains from beating or scolding her, instead approaching her daughter's defence and the potential judgement of neighbours. At the same time, 32-year-old Lila maintains traditional gender divides and rejects Luyando's complaints of having to work hard every day (line 12) while her mother lets the boys stay 'without doing anything' (line 14), telling her 'You want the boys to do this, even though you, a girl, is here? I don't know why you're like that' (line 11) and 'You, a girl, think that boys should wash when you're there' (line 13). As noted, girls and women performed the large majority of housework across Hang'ombe families, and girls were generally subject to much stricter social regulation than boys. Although some parents, especially younger women, lamented this disparity during interviews, they stressed the importance of respecting local customs in order to maintain their family's reputation and basic sustenance. Such concern with the judgement of others is also displayed by Lila above, telling Luyando how 'Nana will hear what we are discussing' and 'this is recording right now' (line 17), referring to the recorder beside them. Interestingly, Luyando seems unaffected by such warnings, maintaining her protest against her mother's commands throughout their interaction above. As a third grader at Mbabala Basic School, Luyando had been taught to interact with teachers on equal footing with boys and to remain critical of social suppression based on class, gender or race. While her parents strongly supported all their children's schooling, they – like other Hang'ombe parents I talked to – revealed fears about how the display of autonomy and lack of accommodation to local customs among young girls like Luyando above might threaten the social position of both the individual girl and her family members.

Although parents were generally much more controlling of young girls than boys, many expressed concern about their teenage sons, who they often found lazy and self-absorbed, spending time with their friends in the local township and neglecting their responsibilities at home. Such defiance was widely associated with the negative influences both boys and girls in the local township were exposed to, as indicated to me by 52-year-old Leonard Hang'ombe below, talking about raising his three teenage grandsons, who stayed with their mother in the homestead of Leonard and his two wives Dorothy and Edinah:

> As a parent and grandparent, I have a big challenge now, teaching my grandsons to survive. They help me plough, but when we come home [from the fields], they just wash and leave and go to the township. As (grand)parents, we must teach our children how to survive through different activities at home, especially these hard years when we're all suffering. But that is a big challenge because children are rarely home, and they disappear right after doing their chores. We [parents and grandparents] did not learn; we did not go to school. But we were taught by our parents how to look after ... to rear chicken, how to plough. Every child must know the basic survival skills, how to keep different kinds of animals at home. So even if you fail at school, you must learn the survival skills at home. The struggle is to send children to school. But even if they fail in school, they must not fail at home. They must learn these household activities so that they can survive. That's why I survive, even if I didn't go to school. Because I learnt these skills.

As I elaborate in Chapter 4, many parents secretly doubted the school's promises of social and financial security, having seen too many young relatives and neighbours return empty-handed after pursuits of employment or higher education in urban areas. Like Leonard, parents thus strongly promoted children's acquisition of basic household and farming skills, which were not only thought to secure their physical survival but also their well-being in a society threatened by moral ambiguity, unimpeded and perhaps even enhanced by the local school. Such parental concern is displayed in the following extract, recorded one evening in January 2009. Love Phiri, a 45-year-old woman and mother of eight children and four grandchildren, was cleaning up the kitchen house along with her youngest daughters, 7-year-old Miyoba and 9-year-old Brenda. The rains had come late that year, and many people were waiting anxiously for their maize to ripen, including Love and her extended family members. Seated by the fire next to Miyoba and Brenda was their 3-year-old cousin John and three of their brothers, Clever (6), Solomon (9) and Julu (11), who were relaxing after a long day of weeding fields with their father. As we enter the conversation below, the children have just finished eating, and Love has just come back from eating in the cikuta to assist the girls in the washing of dishes:

[John makes a crying sound.]

1. Love [jokingly]: Aisya, ino kayi?
   Uncle, what is the matter?

2. John [crying]: Kuli wandikkala.
   Someone has sat on me [my leg].

3. Love [jokingly]: Nguni wakukkala.
   Who has sat on you?

[Laughter from the other children.]

4. Love [to Miyoba]: Mama, sanzya nkapu eyi gusya alya.
   Mama, pick up that cup on the floor and wash it.

[Miyoba picks up the cup and washes it.]

5. Love [to Miyoba]: Leta kuno.
   Bring it here.

6. John: Ndikkale kuli?
   Where should I sit?

7. Brenda [to John]: Ulawida ankendulo.
   You'll fall on the candle.

8. Love [to Julu, annoyed]: Julu, cisyu cali mukapoto wacilya buti cali mukapika? Wagusya alimwi?
   Julu, how much relish did you eat from the pot? Did you get more relish?

9. Julu: Ndagusya buyo kasyoonto.
   I only got very little.

10. Love: Ino wasiya tupiisi tongaye?
    How many pieces [of chicken] did you leave?

11. Julu: Ccita naatwali tongaye nseetubalide.
    I don't know. I didn't count them.

12. Solomon: Kwiina acaceede.
    Nothing was left.

13. Julu [to Solomon, surprised]: Kwiina acaceede?
    Nothing was left?

14. Love: liyi, ccita kuti kuli wazubula.
    Right, unless someone else got the pieces.

15. Julu [defensively]: Andiza kuli watugusya, ndasiya awa mpoonya ndainka.
    Maybe somebody did, because I left the pieces.

16. Brenda: Ngoonya waceede mucikuta buya.
    Whoever stayed in the kitchen ate the pieces.

17. Love [to Julu, angrily]: Kalakuwida kaambo nkaambo boonse ...!
    You are the guilty one because everyone [says so] ...!

18. Julu [to Love, apologetically]: Amunvwe ...
    Listen ...

19. Love [angrily]: Ndajikide kasima kuti bina Luulu a bina Babra balye. Kwajanika buyo tupiisi naatongaye, tobile, totatwe.
    I cooked nsima for Bina Luulu and Bina Babra. When I wanted to give them relish, I found that there were only two–three pieces left.

20. Julu [to Love]: Kwiina ancomwajana?
    You didn't find any pieces?

21. Love [to Julu]: Mpoonya buya kwamana?
    Is that all [you have to say for yourself]?

22. Julu [quietly]: Akakaya kakumamanino.
    I did take an extra piece.

[Love and the children remain silent for a while as the girls continue the cleaning of dishes.]

23. Solomon [to Love]: Eci cisyu cabota.
    This relish has been cooked nicely.

24. Love: Eci cisyu kai? Sunu wacijika mbuli muntu uukkwene.
    This relish? Today she [Brenda] has cooked like a sane person.

25. Solomon [jokingly]: Baama, takkwene na?
    Mother, is she crazy?

[Laughter from Love and the other children.]

26. Love: Inga mbobajika lyoonse, inga maanzi.

> *Most of the time they [my daughters] put too much water [in the relish].*

27. Solomon [jokingly]: Kamuti 'wajika mbuli muntu mupati'.

> *You should say 'she has cooked like a mature person'.*

[Love does not respond to this. After a while, the children all leave to prepare for bed.]

Adults often used the misconduct of an individual child as a source of children's collective moral education, rebuking him or her while including bystanding peers as both witnesses and potential perpetrators. Above, Love keeps commenting on different children's verbal, social and physical conduct, using both humour – e.g. addressing little John with the overly formal *aisya* ('uncle', line 1), which makes all the children laugh – and rigour, rebuking her son Julu for over-eating (lines 8–22) and criticising her daughter Brenda's cooking for being 'full of water' (lines 24–26). As the older brother of six children, 11-year-old Julu has long contributed substantially to the family economy, tending his own cattle, growing his own vegetables and selling them at the weekly market. This endows him with a certain authority among his peers but expectations of social responsibility and maturity have increased. Suspecting Julu for having eaten the relish and chicken she had reserved for some visitors earlier that day, Love interrogates him, rejecting his attempts to defend himself and depicting him as selfish and inconsiderate of the family's current shortage of food (lines 17–19). The bystanding children follow this exchange closely, making meek comments to sustain Love's accusations (lines 12, 16) while trying to avoid moral charges themselves. Relieving the situation, 9-year-old Solomon then compliments his sister Brenda' cooking (line 23), to which Love replies, rather disparaging, that today Brenda has cooked 'like a sane person' (*muntu uukkwene*, line 24). This term regards a person's social intelligence and responsibility, which may be contrasted with *muntu uutakkwene* – that is, a crazy and/or immoral person. Solomon playfully challenges his mother's comment, asking if Brenda 'is crazy' (line 25), which evokes the laughter of both Love and the other children. Love then reminds both Solomon and the others to be diligent in their chores as she criticises her daughters' usual cooking for being 'full of water' (*inga maanzi*, line 26). Still joking, Solomon suggests Love instead use the expression '*muntu mupati*' (mature person, line 27), which contains similar socio-affective traits to *muntu uukkwene* but without the connotations of mental illness. The interaction thus demonstrates the ongoing negotiation and reproduction of generational hierarchies and moral ideals among many Hang'ombe families, involving members of all ages.

In the face of defiant or lazy children, younger women sometimes sought the advice of older, more experienced women, worrying not only about their children's conduct but also about their own skills and estimation as young mothers in local society. This was apparent in a conversation that occurred one early morning in January 2009, when a group of six women from different neighbouring homesteads came to the household of Khama and Minivah's family to help out with the picking of groundnuts: Love (45), Minivah (38), Mila (31), Ruth (38), Modrin (35) and Belita (28), along with Modrin's 8-year-old daughter Eva. The women were all interrelated and quite familiar but also highly respectful of Minivah's sister-in-law Love, who as the oldest in the group and as a successful business women at the local market maintained a strong authority across the community. Present was also Minivah's daughters, 11-year-old Talala and 9-year-old Mududu, quietly assisting the adults. At one point, the women began discussing whether or not a mother should 'chat' (*shimika*) with her daughters – that is, if she should talk openly about other members and events in the community, including delicate issues like sex and romance. As appears below, Love carried strong views on this matter:[3]

1. Belita: Kuti balumi bangu kabatako inga, ndiizya aamwana wangu.
    If my husband isn't home, I chat with my [10-year-old] daughter.

2. Love: Mebo nsesoli kwiizya aamwana.
    I can't chat with a child.

3. Minivah [to Love]: Cilakatazya?
    Is it difficult [for you]?

4. Love: Taciyandiki kwiizya aamwana. Bana nobacili mbuli yooyu, takuyandiki kwizya aambabo.
    It is not advisable to chat with children. When children are of size, you shouldn't chat with them.

5. Minivah: Mebo cilandikatazya nkaambo …
    I have a problem because …

6. Belita: Inga nkubaanina buyo.
    I just tell them stories.

7. Love: Bamwi inga nkwiizya abana, 'Heheeeee Uuuu'.

> *Some chat with their children, 'Heheeeee Uuuu' [mimicking women's chatting].*

[Laughter from all the women.]

8. Love: Mbuyanga. Balandicima bamakaintu baseka boobu abana. Kuti ndakunvwa kuseka Minivah, 'Heheeee Uuuu' a Talala, inga ndati uli muyanga.

> *That's foolish. I hate women who laugh with their children in that way. If I hear you laughing, Minivah, 'Heheeee uuuuu' with Talala, I'll say you're a fool.*

[Laughter from all the women.]

9. Love: Aba beelede kuseka mulicabo.

> *These [children] must chat among themselves.*

10. Women [all]: Iiyi.

> *Yes.*

11. Love: Kuti uyanda kumuyiisya cintu mwana, inga wamuiisya. Wamana ku muyiisya, weelede kugola. Takuyandiki kutalika kuti cili boobu ndakacibona acili boobu.

> *If you want to tell or teach your child something, you should teach her. After teaching her, you must end the talk. It is not a good idea to start telling stories.*

12. Minivah: Bunji bwazyiindi ndaizya abana. Inga balandaambila zyintu nzyobabona, mbuli ku Mbabala.

> *Most of the time, I chat with my children. We talk about things they have seen, for example in Mbabala [Township].*

13. Love: Iiyi, ndabona.

> *Okay, I see.*

14. Minivah: Nceyanda buyo nkuti kabaamba munzila yabulemu. Mbuli kuti, naawaambila ndime at 'Badaala', inga ndamwaambila kuti taciyandiki.

> *What I want from them is to talk to me in a respectful way. For instance, if they address me as 'Man' [Badaala], I tell them that this isn't appropriate.*

[Loud laughter from all the women at the mentioning of the slang expression 'Badaala'.]

15. Love [to all]: Mwabona, mwana teelede kukkala abapati.

> *You see, a child shouldn't sit together with adults.*

16. Minivah: Masimpe?
    Really?

17. Love: Kuti mwana wakkala aabapati, inga watalika kuti kufwumbwa
    nkaanvwa kubapati waakwaambila beenzyina. Inga ainka kukusobana,
    waakwaambila beenzyina nzyobali kwaamba bapati.
    *If a child sits with adults, it'll go out telling friends what it heard
    from the adults. When the child goes playing with friends, it'll
    tell the friends what the adults were talking about.*

18. Minivah: Bunji bwazyiindi, ndaizya abana bangu kapati kuti kuli cimwi
    cintu ca bakatazya, ciyandika kuti ndibapandulwide.
    *Most of the time, I chat with my children, especially if there's
    something they don't understand which they want me to
    explain to them.*

19. Love: Iiyi, taciyandiki kwiizya abana kakwiina akaambo.
    Okay, it's not advisable to chat with children without a purpose.

[The women remain quiet for a while after this.]

Teasing each other, laughing and exchanging personal experiences,
these women appear outspoken in a way rarely seen in the company
of husbands, fathers, adult sons or other men. During my longer visits
to different Hang'ombe families, I often noticed how both younger
and older women in interaction would lower their voices and speak
more discretely if their husbands or other adult males approached
them, while resuming to speak louder and more frankly once there
were no adult men present again. Such social accommodation may
be explained by women's general fear of being labelled bunkanwe or
'gossipy', as described before, associating women's social and linguistic
conduct with wider moral concerns. The women above thus show
a strong concern with their daughters' behaviour, along with their
own conduct as educators and female role models. Different practices
appear to prevail in different homes, with some women interacting
more intimately with their daughters than others. 28-year-old Belita
confesses to 'chatting' with her 10-year-old daughter whenever her
husband is not at home (line 1). Love rejects this practice (line 2),
denoting it as 'not advisable' and 'foolish' (lines 4, 8), especially when
children 'are of size' – that is, from around the age of ten. As noted
earlier, older women, especially those with little formal schooling like
Love, tended to retain a strict authority towards their children and
often promoted such authority to their female friends and relatives.
Concerned not only with their daughters' social appearance but

also their own, older women might utilise a social gathering like the above to assert themselves as examples to their younger peers, thus maintaining some respect and legitimacy in times of changing ideals. With statements like 'A child should not sit together with adults' (line 15), 'It is not advisable to chat with children without a purpose' (line 19) and gently ridiculing her 38-year-old sister-in-law Minivah for chatting with her 11-year-old daughter Talala (line 8), Love thus asserts her moral authority in the group above. The extract reveals the local power of moral discourse, creating bonds and directions in an atmosphere of social upheaval.

Confiding in Grandparents

If children lived with or in near proximity of grandparents, these often served as softer, more elaborate authorities and caretakers than parents. As in other parts of Africa, the social relationships between approximate and alternating generations differed quite distinctly among Hang'ombe families, the latter allowing for a wider social latitude (Geissler and Prince 2004). A granddaughter might jokingly be addressed by her grandfather as 'my wife' (*mukaintu wangu*) and by her grandmother as 'co-wife' (*mukazyima*), disarming common sexual and incestuous taboos. Paradoxically, the indisputable respect of elders ascribed them with a wider moral leeway, and older children's introduction to sensitive issues and taboos around sexuality, witchcraft, alcohol etc. was often passed on by their grandparents. Like older siblings, especially grandmothers thus often served as central agents of children's socialisation, enabling their early social and linguistic experiments.

After their parents' divorce Eden, Nchimunya and their 10-year-old brother Banda went to live with their maternal grandparents in the Phiri munzi – along with their eight first and second cousins and their respective parents and grandparents, who stayed in two other households within the homestead – while their mother moved to her new husband's village. In the extract below, 64-year-old Elizabeth is sitting with her two grandchildren, 3-year-old Eden and 7-year-old Nchimunya, in the family's mutual kitchen one evening in December 2008. Elizabeth asks Nchimunya to go look for Banda, who has run off to spend time with his friends in the township several days before (lines 1, 4). Notably, Elizabeth urges Nchimunya to persuade Banda to come home rather than threaten him with a beating, which might be the typical parental response to such a misdeed. Further on, Elizabeth asks

Nchimunya about the work efforts of her neighbour Mrs Lamwiilo, who is the widow of a man named Chester and respectfully referred to as *Bamuka Chester* or 'Chester's wife' (lines 7, 9). Since she has no close relatives living nearby and has not yet been invited to the homes of one of her sons, Bamuka Chester largely relies on her own work efforts. The issues of Banda's escape and Bamuka Chester's self-sustenance could both be seen as highly sensitive, evoking themes of vulnerability and intergenerational conflict. As appears below, however, Elizabeth addresses these issues quite openly to her young grandson, allowing a confidentiality unlikely to occur between parents and children:[4]

1. Elizabeth: Nchimunya, kaka ufwume juunza ukeete mwana uutako.

    Nchimunya, please go tomorrow morning and bring home the absent child.

2. Eden: Banda?

    Banda?

3. Nchimunya [to Eden]: Kolemeka.

    Show respect [by saying 'Ba Banda'].

4. Elizabeth [to Nchimunya]: *Ukamukombelezya. Ukamukombelezye kuboola. Ukamwaambile kuti: 'Tiye, kung'anda'. Uyoozumina. Kuli wakandaambila kuti wakamubona ku Mbabala a nyama ya ngulube. Wakaamba kuti ulaboola, nkaambo ulipengede.*

    Try to persuade him [Banda] to come home. Tell him 'Let's go home'. He'll agree. Someone told me they saw him with pork meat in the township. He said he was coming home because he has a problem.

5. Nchimunya: Nguni wakwaambila? Ngu Mwila?

    Who told you [about Banda]? Was it Mwila?

6. Elizabeth [to Nchimunya]: *Ndali mulubide.*

    I forgot [who told me].

    [Elizabeth and the children remain silent for a while.]

7. Elizabeth: Nsezyi naabagolela aali Bamuka Chester sunu.

    I don't know how much work Chester's wife did today.

8. Nchimunya: Tiibalima maningi sunu.

    She didn't weed much today.

9. Elizabeth: Sena wabona mpobagolela?

    Did you see where she finished?

10. Nchimunya: Inga mbuli kuti tiibalimina mumwi.
    It seems she didn't weed certain areas.

11. Elizabeth: Kweelede kubelesya nkolobeki.
    She should use a plough.

Elizabeth approaches her grandson as a trusted interlocutor, implicitly sharing her concerns about Banda (line 4) and her widowed neighbour (line 11). Likewise, 7-year-old Nchimunya responds to his grandmother almost as an equal, asking her the source of information about Banda (line 5) and making his own assessments of Bamuka Chester's work efforts (line 8, 10). Conversations between children and their grandparents did not always concern sensitive issues, but they often emitted an intimacy seemingly appreciated by both parts. In terms of the 10-year-old runaway Banda, the fact that Elizabeth does not try to threaten him to come home but rather asks Nchimunya to persuade him (line 4) appears to reflect such closeness, even if Elizabeth remains the main authority in Banda's current life. Kinship studies have shown how altering migration patterns and the advent of HIV/Aids have affected grandparents' position in many African families in the past decades, forcing them to take on the restrictive roles and responsibilities normally ascribed to parents (Alber, Van der Geest and Whyte 2008). This might also be the case in some Hang'ombe families afflicted by disease and poverty or parents' divorce. However, even in such families, I generally observed intimate relationships between grandparents and children, like between Elizabeth and her grandchildren above. This did not mean that children generally lacked respect for elders, however, which was visible, for example, in Nchimunya's directive to his younger sister Eden about 'showing respect' when addressing her grandmother (line 3). Likewise, in his last comment on the sparse weeding job of Bamuka Chester, Nchimunya avoids making any condescending remarks, using the suggestive expression *inga mbuli* or 'you might think' (line 10) – an expression he is unlikely to use towards a peer.

Listening to Adults' Talk

Assisting with work in the fields and within households, Hang'ombe children generally had a broad exposure to the daily concerns expressed by adult family members, including marketplace chatter and family talk around household fires. As long as they remained quiet and discrete about the insights they might acquire, children were rarely told to leave. Gossip about neighbours and relatives was a favoured activity, most people having known each other for decades or been familiarised through church or intermarriage. At one point during my stay in 2008–9, many families were concerned with the case of Eden, a 38-year-old well-respected local woman, who was caught stealing in the larger town of Choma. Eden's husband had recently stopped supporting her and their three children in favour of a younger wife, allegedly causing Eden to travel to Choma and steal clothes and other necessities for herself and her family. The incident caused quite a stir and evoked both disdain and sympathy among fellow community members, especially as Eden was forced by the senior headman to carry a big sign saying 'big thief' (*kabwalala mupati*) around her neck for several days. A similar case happened in early 2009, when the 82-year-old grandfather in the family I was staying with, Benson Hang'ombe, fell very ill and needed to be hospitalised immediately. This was no simple matter, as there was little access to the transport necessary to carry a sick older man the 50 km to the nearest hospital, and also Benson would need constant assistance for several days, possibly weeks, once he arrived. According to local conventions, solving a family crisis like this was the responsibility of the oldest son, or, in case of insuperable distances, the oldest son living nearby (Cliggett 2001, 2003). In this particular situation, finding transport, paying the driver and accompanying Benson and his wife Sarah to the hospital were the obvious responsibilities of their older son Citumbo, who lived with his family right by Benson's homestead. However, on the morning when Benson and Sarah were supposed to leave for the hospital, Citumbo went to his maize field like any other day, seemingly unaware of his family obligations. A younger brother had to go and 'remind' him of these, much to the regret of both Benson and his many relatives, who had come to sympathise and pray for the old man. According to Citumbo's wife Joyce, who came around later that day to express a harsh disapproval of her husband's 'cowardly behaviour' (*micito yabukandu*), this evasion was rooted in Citumbo's fear of interaction with educated people like the clinical personnel, having had only four years of formal schooling. He also had hearing difficulties in one ear. Citumbo seemed to feel inferior and timid during conversations with more educated people, who were likely to use words and concepts unfamiliar to him. As had been the case before, Citumbo's improper conduct caused a heavy stir among his immediate and extended family members, who felt humiliated in front of neighbouring families. In the end, Citumbo was subtly but effectively forced to fulfil his obligations, arranging a vehicle, paying the driver and other expenses and spending the subsequent weeks with his parents at the hospital.

Family talk often centred on the negligence or misfortune of neighbours and relatives like Eden and Citumbo, lamenting society's general decay. Such lamenting was common not only among elders but also younger adults, as the following extract reveals. One night in January 2009, Khama (27), his sister Minivah (38) and their male cousin Sinyimbwe (20) were relaxing together around the fire in the family's cikuta while chatting with Minivah and Khama's nephew Talis (28), who had recently arrived from Livingston to stay with the family for a longer period. Quietly eavesdropping on their conversation were Minivah's five children, Talala (11), Mududu (9), Lushomo (8), Habeenzu (3), Lweendo (1), and myself. Minivah and Khama's older parents had been away for a few days visiting the nearby hospital, perhaps allowing the younger adults a more open exchange than usual. At one point in the conversation, Sinyimbwe referred to a recent wedding between a local 16-year-old girl and a man from another Zambian region. This evoked a wider discussion on the alleged lowering of marital and maternity age for young women and the increasing number of male workers arriving from other regions. At the time of recording, the extensive tarring of the Namwala Road passing through Hang'ombe had gone on for about a year, during which the road workers – most of whom belonged to the Bemba tribe, accused locally of being arrogant and thievish – had been known to spend their limited salary on beer and prostitutes in Mbabala Township, close by the village. Some workers had married or formed sexual relations with young women from surrounding villages, much to the disdain of many members:

1. Sinyimbwe: Umwi taakasamide masookesi amucado wakwe.
   Someone didn't wear socks on his wedding day.

2. Minivah: Nguni?
   Who?

3. Sinyimbwe: Uya mwaalumi wakakwata kwa Mylon.
   The man who married at Mylon's home.

4. Minivah: Taakasamide masookesi?
   He didn't wear socks?

5. Sinyimbwe: Wakali samide pesi akali kulangika mbuli lukanda. Inga ulati *ndukanda*.
   He was wearing socks, but they looked like skin. You'd think it was the skin.

6. Khama: Nguni wakali kukwata?

> *Who got married?*

7. Minivah: Mwana waba Mylon nguwakakwatwa. Ati nguni zyina mwana uya, Talala?

> *Mylon's daughter married some man. What is the name of the daughter, Talala?*

8. Talala: Odria.

> *Odria [a 16-year-old girl from Hang'ombe].*

9. Khama [surprised]: Odria wakakwatwa?

> *Odria got married?*

10. Sinyimbwe and Talala: Iiyi.

> *Yes.*

11. Sinyimbwe: Ano mazuba bantu balafwambaana kukwata … Ano mazuba bantu balafwambaana kukwata.

> *Nowadays, people marry early … Nowadays, people marry early.*

12. Minivah: Basimbi balafwambaana kukwatwa. Balamita olo balafwambaana kukwatwa.

> *Young girls marry yearly. They either get pregnant or marry early.*

13. Talis: Bantu babeleka kuma Chinise mbobanyonganya bana basimbi.

> *The people working for the Chinese are spoiling young girls.*

14. Sinyimbwe: Bainka bama Chinise, tulayoya. Bababweza basimbi boonse.

> *When the Chinese go, we will relax. They have taken all the girls.*

15. Minivah: Bainka, balasiya banyonyoona cisi.

> *Before they go, they will have destroyed our society.*

16. Sinyimbwe: Bana basimbi balamana kufwa malwazi.

> *Young girls will die of diseases.*

17. Talis: Kamulangilila buyo, aatimanine six years, basimbi banji banoofwide.

> *Just keep your eyes open. After six years, most of the young girls will be dead.*

18. Sinyimbwe: Bamwi [basimbi] tabacizyi kujika.
    Some of them [the young girls] don't know how to cook.

19. Minivah: Kujika talili penzi kuti muntu kajisi mali.
    Cooking is not a problem if one has money.

20. Talis: Mali aubyaubya zyintu.
    Money makes things easy.

21. Minivah: Aba bana bakwatwa balakwatwa nkaambo balizyi kuti banookkuta bakwatwa.
    These young girls getting married do so because they know they'll have enough food in marriage.

Besides entertainment, such exchanges might serve to soothe actors' experiences of uncertainty and assert their own moral decency, as they settled conventions, for example, for dress (wearing socks and other kinds of civilised clothing on one's wedding day, lines 1–5) and girls' proper marital age (later than sixteen, lines 7–12). The moral education of young girls was frequently brought up in such family talks and often linked to exterior threats like the Bemba road workers 'spoiling young girls' (line 13) and 'destroying society' (line 15), a threat entailing other negative influences, like HIV / Aids, unemployment, alcoholism, early pregnancies and young people's alleged disrespect of older traditions (lines 13–18). At the same time, exterior influences were widely seen as necessary to local society, including schooling, money flows and improved living standards, like Minivah and Talis agreeing on how 'cooking is not a problem if one has money' (line 19) and 'money makes things easy' (line 20). As Minivah notes, a young girl might marry or get pregnant by a wealthy road worker in the hope of a more comfortable and relatively secure family life than if marrying a local farmer (line 21). However, such conduct was likely to expose both the girl and her family to massive judgement, and so most parents sought to prevent their daughters from getting involved with foreigners, either Bemba or Chinese.

From a linguistic-anthropological approach, the last half of the interaction above (lines 11–21) is noteworthy in the way the four speakers repeat and extend each other's utterances, thus aligning themselves around the experience of negative foreign influences and a general moral decay. Such repetitive or complementary speech was common among the adult villagers I observed – younger and older alike – forming experiences of consensus and alignment among family and community members. Anthropologists Alber, Van der

Geest and Whyte (2008) note how especially older members in many rural African societies have been heard complaining about the present and idealising the past – a so-called *complaint discourse* through which they might counter 'the experience of being marginalised today, through the workings of historical forces or personal neglect and mistreatment from their children and grandchildren' (Alber, Van der Geest and Whyte 2008: 10). This was also the case among many Hang'ombe elders, immersing themselves in ongoing complaints about current affairs while reminiscing a better, morally superior past. In line with the family talk above, Alber et al. have observed such complaint discourse and past idealisation among younger Africans as well, using it 'as a way out of present difficulties to a better future. Tradition becomes a way of opposing the generation of their parents, who are construed as having betrayed it' (ibid.: 11). Compared to their parents and grandparents, who in their own accounts grew up in socially and economically solid communities while at the same time experiencing Zambia's 'golden age' of rapid economic and infrastructural development from 1965 to the mid 1970s, younger villagers like Minivah, Khama, Sinyimbwe and Talis shared the experience of a more threatening and uncertain future, providing few obvious pathways to social and financial security. Countering such uncertainty, younger villagers might seek to aspire to each other's level of optimism and moral support by – like their parents and grandparents – collectively construing a more ideal past.

Children eavesdropping on family talks as legitimate or candid listeners, like Talala, Mududu, Lushomo and Habeenzu above, were likely to observe the social power of moral discourse and complaint, connecting members and establishing experiences of security and dignity in a life many people saw as strenuous and demeaning. Few people had access to basic commodities like electricity or running water, and almost everyone had lost close friends or family members to disease or malnourishment. Basic household security might quickly be ambushed by a husband leaving his wife and children for another woman, or a family member falling ill and needing expensive healthcare. Asserting themselves as righteous beings in the midst of such challenges, villagers maintained a strong moral discourse and appearance, keeping themselves and their homes immaculate while continuously reminding each other of the proper way to live and act. As I elaborate in the next chapter, children drew heavily on adults' moral discourse among their peers, imitating, mimicking and mocking their solemn speech.

Conclusion

Overall, Hang'ombe children grew up in an environment marked by a mixture of moral idealism and pragmatic perseverance. From an early age, they entered a collective workforce, prompting them to become skilful contributors to their family households and be deeply immersed in the doings and concerns of both their peers and family members. Raising their families against the drawback of economic globalisation – financial instability, a fluctuating, highly competitive job market and the experience of increasing socio-economic marginalisation – most parents sought to secure themselves and their children through the transmission of manual labour and traditional family ideals of collectivity and respect. Observing the weakening of such ideals, some villagers pursued more opportunistic ventures like marrying an employed foreigner at a young age, engaging with a married patron, entering a shady business deal or stealing clothes from a commercial store. The lack of physical boundaries across homesteads and their access to practically all arenas of the local community ensured that children were broadly exposed to the adult world, giving them mixed messages of 'normal' or proper personhood. Conflict between formal discourse and tangible everyday conduct may exist in all places and levels of society, and most parents recognise the challenge of abiding by their own demands to children. But in a society where parents rarely sit down and talk with children more elaborately, children are left to deal with such conflicts and ambiguities largely on their own. Hang'ombe parents and adult siblings offered plenty of guidance, enrolling children in their daily work chores and telling them how or how not to speak and act in different arenas, but they rarely addressed more sensitive issues like money, sex, alcohol, friendship or schooling, even with adolescents. Parents tried to prepare children for a life sustained by diligent labour and social reciprocity, much like their own, and to shield them from social influences that might threaten this sustenance. But realising the infeasibility of safeguarding them in a close-knit society relying closely on their participation in practically all aspects of daily community life, many parents – especially younger ones – assumed a more pragmatic approach, accepting children's increasing familiarity with the social ambiguities of modern life. As I reveal in the following chapter, Hang'ombe children displayed a pronounced ability to intercept such ambiguities around them and to process and extract their creative social potential.

Notes

1. I observed and recorded this interaction while sitting on a stool by the kitchen wall.
2. Shadrik carried the recorder in his shirt pocket while driving the plough and whipping the oxen. Clever remained at his father's side throughout the two-hour ploughing of this particular patch, which I observed from a path nearby.
3. Minivah held the recorder in her pocket during the interaction above while I observed the women from a small distance.
4. This recording was made by the family themselves one evening in early February 2009.

Hang'ombe homestead and surrounding fields. Photograph by the author.

Talala and Benson in the *cikuta* or visitor's hall. Photograph by the author.

Mbabala Basic School. Photograph by the author.

Grade seven, English class at Mbabala Basic School. Photograph by the author.

Four cousins on their way to school. Photograph by the author.

Lushomo with Lweendo in the garden. Photograph by the author.

Father and son ploughing. Photograph by the author.

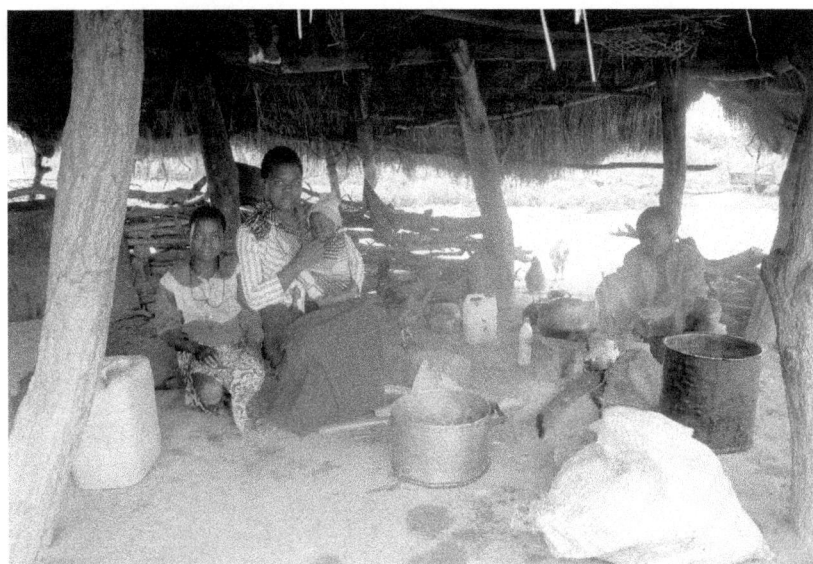

A mother and her children by the kitchen fire. Photograph by the author.

Research assistant Khama Hang'ombe. Photograph by the author.

The author (right) with Khama, Minivah, Lweendo and Habeenzu by the guest house. Photograph by the author.

❧ 3

'Is That How You Insult in Your House?'

Linguistic Agency among Hang'ombe Children

> I teach my [younger] sister and brother to show respect to elders and not to use insults. They learn by hearing the way I speak to them.
> —Ines, 8-year-old girl

> The children in the township are worse than us. They lie and curse, and sometimes they fight, even if their parents are there.
> —Richwel, 9-year-old boy

One Tuesday afternoon in May 2009, four children were walking home from school: 10-year-old Banda and his cousins Julu (11), Brenda (9) and Miyoba (7). Having grown up in different households within the Phiri homestead – Banda with his grandmother and two younger siblings in one household, Julu, Brenda and Miyoba with their parents and brothers in another – the children shared a close familiarity while at the same time experiencing different parental routines. This evoked frequent discussions among the children on rules and leeways, comparing and classifying each other's observations. While walking home this particular afternoon, Banda and Julu began sharing their experiences of watching TV. Miyoba then reported having watched TV the previous night with the children's 20-year-old cousin Obrian, who was widely known – and whose younger peers were somewhat in awe of him – for disregarding general norms of respectability, including with his own family members:

1. Banda [to Julu]: Balakasya kutamba banyoko na?
   Does your mother prohibit you to watch [TV]?

2. Julu: Iiyi. Balakasya kuti kabakkede aaba taata. Inga tutamba bainka kukulala. Mu nsabata inga tutamba 'Kantuunya Kamu Nsabata'.

> *Yes. She does if she is watching with father. We [children] watch when they go to bed. On Saturdays we watch a Tonga programme called 'The Saturday Play'.*

3. Miyoba [to Julu]: Ede jilo wakafwambaana kulala. Ndakali kutamba aa Obrian.

> *But yesterday you went to bed early. I watched with Obrian.*

4. Julu: Ndijilo buyo. Lyoonse inga ndime eecaalizya kutamba.

> *That was only yesterday. All these other days I keep watching while you go to bed.*

5. Brenda: Obrian bakamukasya kutamba alikke ati inga waisambala TV.

> *Obrian was told not to watch alone as he might sell the TV.*

6. Banda: Iiyi uyooibba. Uyooisambala.

> *Yes, he'll steal it. He'll sell it.*

7. Miyoba [to Banda]: Ulakuuma kuti akunvwe. Ndamwaambila.

> *He'll beat you if he hears you. I'll tell him.*

8. Banda [to Miyoba]: Ndakuuma!

> *I'll beat you!*

9. Julu: Juunza ndime eembela. Bwali bulizyi bwa Obrian. Ati ulandipa mali.

> *Tomorrow I'll be the one looking after cattle. It was Obrian's turn. He said he'd pay me.*

10. Miyoba: Ino kucikolo?

> *What about school?*

11. Julu: Juunza tatwiiyi.

> *Tomorrow we're not learning [going to school].*

12. Banda: Mebo juunza ndiyoomuka kubuka. Ndiyanda kuti nkapumune.

> *Tomorrow I'll wake up late. I want to rest.*

13. Brenda: Ndilafwambaana koona tufwumina ku garden.

> *I'll wake up early because we're going to the garden.*

14. Banda [to Julu]: Ino Obrian uya kuli walo?

> *Where is Obrian going?*

15. Julu: Ati uya kubbola. Pesi bataata bakandikasya kumweembelela
nkaambo ulasyupa kupa mali.

> *He said he was going to play football. But father told me never
> to take care of the animals on his behalf because he is difficult
> to pay [he rarely returns the favour].*

16. Banda: Ino uyoocita buti?

> *What are you going to do?*

17. Julu: Tabakandiboni bafwumina ku garden.

> *He [my father] will not know [that I'm looking after the cattle]
> because he's going to the garden in the morning.*

18. Banda: Julu konvwa kwaambilwa kuti bakukasya nkuleka.

> *Julu, you should obey. If they [your parents] said you shouldn't,
> then you shouldn't.*

19. Brenda: Alimwi ndabaambila kuti uyanda kweembelela Obrian. Obrian
ulabeja tainki kubbola uya kutusimbi olo kukubba.

> *I'll tell them [our parents] you're looking after the cattle on
> Obrian's behalf. Obrian is lying that he's going to play football;
> he is either going to see his girlfriend or go stealing.*

20. Miyoba: Obrian eliya wakabba mali aabanene. Ulabba.

> *Obrian stole grandmother's money last time. He is a thief.*

21. Banda: Nciconya eci ncobaleka cikolo, nkubba.

> *This is a result of stopping school, stealing.*

> *[The children stay quiet for a brief while.]*

22. Banda: Julu inga mulatamba TV?

> *Julu, do you normally watch TV?*

23. Julu: Iiyi tulatamba inga.

> *Yes, we do.*

24. Miyoba: Ndime nditamba maningi.

> *I watch more [than both of you].*

25. Banda [annoyed, to Miyoba]: Kayi nzyokonzya zyalo ezyo. Kukkala
buyo akulya.

> *That is what you know best. To just sit and eat.*

26. Brenda: Inga tutamba 'Kantuunya Kamu Nsabata' a 'Hamaleke'.

> *We watch 'The Saturday Play' and 'Hamaleke'.*

27. Julu: 'Hamaleke' nimbotu.
    'Hamaleke' is nice.

28. Miyoba: A news inga tulatamba.
    We also watch the news.

29. Julu: Tutamba yakumazuba, yacikuwa inga ili masiku.
    We watch the [local] evening news; the news in English comes at night.

30. Miyoba: Yoonse badaala.
    We watch all the news.

31. Banda [to Miyoba]: Cikuwa inga cilanjila oku akuzwa oku.
    English comes in through this [your] ear and goes out through the other.

32. Miyoba [upset]: Zwa awa!
    Get out!

33. Brenda: Iiyi inga tulanvwa yamucikuwa.
    Yes, we [also] listen to news in English.

34. Julu [to Brenda]: Ootanvwi cikuwa. Inga upwaya buyo meso.
    You don't understand English. You only watch the pictures.

35. Brenda: Ubona nduwe ocidalu. Swebo inga tulinvwide. Miyoba tweende tubasiye bolikke basimulomo.
    I'm not slow like you. I understand. [To Miyoba] Miyoba, let's go. Let's leave these who are gossipy.

36. Julu [angrily]: Kamuya. Bayoomutanda munganda munyane mubone. Mulayanda kukkala aabapati.
    You leave. You will be chased out the house and you'll be shamed for it. You like being with adults.

[The two girls leave, and Banda leaves shortly after that.]

Between my visits to Hang'ombe in 2008 and 2010, the number of households possessing a battery-driven television set rose from about 5 per cent to 25 per cent, altering basic routines in many families. From chatting about current events and themes, mostly seated in different areas of the homestead – that is, women and children around kitchen fires, men and older boys in main houses or on the cikuta floor – members across gender and age increasingly spent evening hours seated closely together on chairs or rugs, quietly watching televised news or entertainment programmes. The relatively recent introduction of TV sets to Hang'ombe households made them an obvious object of children's interest, sharing both tangible features and parental regulations on viewing. Many adults feared children's exposure to immoral content, like sex or violence, and so they sought to prevent them from watching, at least in the company of their fathers. When I asked parents, many told me they suspected their children sneak into the main house and turn on the TV late at night, something they regretted but also quietly accepted, saying 'What can we do?'

Such parental concern was justified in exchanges such as those between Julu and his peers above, proudly revealing their candid TV viewing to their male cousin Banda (lines 1–4, 22–34). Excited by the breaking of rules and accessing confidential and somewhat exotic knowledge, the children both seek to surpass each other and explore the wider social repercussions of watching TV late at night. Miyoba thus challenges Julu, telling him 'Yesterday you went to bed early' while she stayed up watching with her older cousin Obrian (line 3) – a claim Julu both confirms and contests, telling Miyoba how he watches 'all these other days' while she sleeps (lines 4). Later on, Julu confirms to Banda how he 'frequently' watches TV (lines 22–23), to which Miyoba comments that she watches 'more' (line 24). Brenda reveals her familiarity with the two weekly chiTonga-spoken entertainment and news programmes, which were both highly popular in the community, *Kantuunya Kamu Nsabata* (*The Saturday Play*) and 'Hamaleke', screened every day at 5 PM (line 26). As appears, watching TV formed a prestigious activity among children, which they used to assert themselves as both courageous – defying parental rules – and as modern and educated, appreciating complex international news coverage.

These associations seemed particularly strong in terms of English-spoken TV programmes, both among children and adults. Although the general proficiency of English was quite low, also among adults with higher levels of education, a high number of villagers watched or reported watching English-spoken programmes. 7-year-old Miyoba reports how she and her family watch 'every news', including the English-spoken news programmes dominating Zambia's two national broadcasting stations, TV1 and TV2 (line 30). Banda taunts her, saying 'English comes in through this ear and goes out through the other' (line 31), to which she sneers back, 'Get out!' (line 32). Julu tells Brenda 'You don't understand English. You only watch the pictures' (line 34), to which Brenda responds that she, unlike Julu, is not 'slow' (*budalu*) but actually understands the English-spoken content. Underlining her superior status, Brenda then tells Miyoba, 'Let's leave these who are gossipy' (line 35). Thus accused of being both slow and morally dubious, Julu warns Brenda that she will be 'chased out the house' and 'shamed' by family members for her inclination to 'be with adults', in spite of their prohibitions (line 36).

The children thus reveal a close familiarity with the status parameters of English vs. chiTonga prevailing in local society, along with their parents' ambiguities around modern commodities like TVs and traditional codices of intergenerational distance and respect. Few children might be permanently 'chased out of the house' for peeking in on parents' TV watching as suggested by Julu above (line 36), but being 'shamed' or socially excluded formed a substantial threat to all. The children's shared concern with the rather tarnished reputation of Obrian, their 20-year-old cousin (lines 5–9, 14–21), reveals a mutual fear and fascination with the possibility of exceeding the extended family unit, a possibility containing both incalculable freedom and loss. When Miyoba proudly reports having watched TV with Obrian the preceding night (line 3), Brenda notes how Obrian has been 'told not to watch alone as he might sell the TV' (line 5), which Banda confirms matter-of-factly, 'Yes, he [Obrian] will steal it. He will sell it' (line 6). When Julu reveals having agreed to replace Obrian in the herding of the family's cattle the following day against payment – thus transgressing his father's warnings (lines 9, 15, 17) – Banda tells him, 'Julu, you should obey. If they [your parents] said you shouldn't, then you shouldn't' (line 18) and is immediately supported by Brenda (line 19). Miyoba first defends Obrian, telling Banda 'He'll beat you if he hears you. I'll tell him' (line 7) but later notes how 'Obrian stole grandmother's money last time. He is a thief' (line 20). From a language socialisation perspective, this exchange may be seen as the children appropriating adults' moral discourse, condemning and disassociating themselves from the misdemeanours of others as they have heard parents and other adults do. Testing different stances and discursive means among each other, they explore the ambiguous, sometimes contradictive social landscape presented to them, establishing their own rules and hierarchies in this landscape. In his apparent disregard of basic social orders, Obrian represents a powerful and somewhat intriguing ally to a 10-year-old boy like Julu, who maintains a relatively low position in the family hierarchy. As appears, however, such an alliance might easily be thwarted by observant peers, using powerful discourses and alignments to maintain or renegotiate the internal hierarchy among them. In his final comment on Obrian, Banda appropriates a common discourse on the moral significance of schooling, noting how 'This [Obrian's tendency to steal] is a result of stopping school, stealing' (line 21). As a 9-year-old second grader, Banda is unlikely to grasp the full social and psychological aspects of this correlation, but like other kinds of moral discourse, it serves him to maintain authority among his peers.

Language socialisation studies have shown how children's interactions and play activities with peers offer important arenas for their exploration of social power structures and dynamics prevailing around them (Goodwin and Kyratzis 2012; Paugh 2005). In the absence of monitoring adults, children may try on different roles and registers to impress, entertain, challenge or control each other, capitalising on the powers ascribed to authoritative figures in their surroundings, like parents, teachers, doctors, policemen, preachers or news broadcasters. Children may also mock such authoritative figures among peers, exaggerating their solemn speech or dramatic gestures, thus subverting existing hierarchies and creating 'alternative social realities in which *they* hold the positions of authority, power, and control, and in doing so, they may also challenge and transform those realities' (Paugh 2005: 65, original emphasis). In her language socialisation study of play activities among a group of 4–5-year-old American preschool girls, Amy Kyratzis shows how the girls negotiate and establish a hierarchical order among each other through their enactment of powerful roles and scenarios like news reporting and prince-princess dating. Depending on the different children's performative skills and creativity, the power balance may fluctuate and change as the rules of the scenario are renegotiated or new characters and positions are enacted (Kyratzis 2007). Children's play activities may thus provide rich ethnographic entries into their understandings of and active attempts to interfere with and utilise the adult worlds presented to them in daily life. As Ann-Carita Evaldsson writes in her overview of language socialisation studies of peer play in both Western and majority settings,

> the variations in play themes and the different ways children organize family and work play across settings point to play as an integral process of children's understanding of family and work, and show that play prepares children for future family and working lives. Thus, ethnographic studies of how children organize play activities across cultures demonstrate the fluidity between play and work, and the intertwining of children's play and the adult world. (Evaldsson 2009: 323)

In my observation, such employment of adult practices not only occurs in children's play activities but also in their conversations and discussions with peers, like the interaction between Banda, Julu, Miyoba and Brenda above. In this chapter, I thus explore Hang'ombe children's use of different social and discursive strategies in their sibling-kin interactions and play activities, employing power structures, roles and scenarios available to them in daily life as a means of social organisation within the peer group, along with testing and challenging local hierarchies and ideals.

Knowing How to Play

Hang'ombe children spent most of their out-of-school time within or in near proximity of their home, and many of their interactions explored basic household concerns. If not busy working, they argued about the distribution and performance of chores, and even while relaxing at home, they discussed crops, animals, foods and weather conditions, gossiped about family or community members, evaluated each other's work performances or mimicked parents' rebukes. While siblings and kin of bother genders often mixed and interacted freely during such periods of relaxation, girls and boys often displayed different orientations in both their speech and play activities that might be read as their early acquisition of gendered roles. I thus often observed younger boys playing 'oxcart' (*cikkoci*), whipping each other or perhaps a dog, telling it to 'speed up' (*kuzuzya*) or 'go in front!' (*kozolola!*), while young girls tended to focus on cooking, washing and other household chores in their peer talk and play activities. Such early experiments with gendered roles and work practices correlate with child psychologist Marianne Bloch's studies in the late 1980s among Lebou families in western Senegal, where she observed boys as young as two years old 'hunting' across the courtyard, while girls mostly imitated the various domestic chores of their mothers and older sisters. Bloch denotes such activities *play-work*, emphasising how children's play activities intersect with ideologies and behavioural norms prevailing around them, including gender (Bloch 1989). As language socialisation scholar Ann-Carita Evaldsson notes, however, 'studies on gender in childhood tend to exaggerate differences. "A strategy of contrasts" is often built into the design of research that constructs and makes only gender differentiation visible' (Evaldsson 2009: 324, quoting Thorne 1993). The children I studied were clearly tuned into gendered roles and ideologies, but I also observed plenty of power struggles and alliances across gender in their interactions with siblings and kin, and girls appeared just as confident and powerful as boys during such interactions. While recognising the social significance and inhibitions of local gender ideologies, I thus perceive gender as one of several social stratification parameters employed and negotiated in Hang'ombe children's peer interactions, including age, modernity and education. As an example of such negotiation, the following interaction was recorded in the Mweemba homestead one dry afternoon in late April 2009. 6-year-old Emma, her 9-year-old sister Luyaba and their 9-year-old cousin Brian were relaxing together in the courtyard, looking after Brian's younger brothers John (3) and Gary (5) while all the adults and older children were busy reaping maize in the nearby fields. Before leaving, Brian's mother Irene had given them some groundnuts and fresh sugarcane to snack on, sternly directing the children to share equally among each other. This evoked some discussion among the five children:[1]

1. Emma [to John]: Utanoobbi nyemu. Ajanza aajanza.

    You shouldn't steal groundnuts. You have groundnuts in both hands.

2. John [to Emma]: Ndakuuma!

    I'll beat you!

3. Luyaba [to Emma]: Ati watibbe munsale. Kulanga ndabweza buyo mpingwa zyongaye one, two, three. Yebo wabweza zyongaye, zyotatwe ayooyo ngoyupa zyo tatwe mebo ndabweza buyo zyobilo.

    She [Brian's mother Clarence] said that I wanted to steal sugarcane. I just got one, two, three pieces. You [Emma] got three plus the one you're eating. I only got two.

4. Emma: Eyi nintengaanetenga.

    This one [sugarcane] isn't ripe.

5. Luyaba: Baliinvwi banyina balikuyeeya kuti inga ndamunyengelela mwana wabo. Bamana bautyola munsale wangu kwiina awabambila.

    His [Brian's] mother was waiting [for Brian to finish eating the sugarcane]; she thought I was going to eat her child's sugarcane. She broke my sugar cane [in two], but I hadn't asked her to do that.

6. Brian [to Luyaba]: Ndakwaambila [kuti utaulyi munsale wangu].

    I told you [not to eat my sugarcane].

7. John [to Luyaba]: Tinka, Tinka.

    Tinka, Tinka.

8. Luyaba: Nguni ngoita kuti 'Tinka'?
   Who are you calling 'Tinka'?

9. John [inaudible]: _____

10. Luyaba [laughing]: Ambaula kabotu.
    Speak properly.

11. John [laughing]: Kayanga-yanga.
    You're foolish.

12. Luyaba [sternly]: Embo mboambaula obo, amabaula kabotu.
    That's not the way you [should] talk, talk properly.

13. John [imitating Luyaba]: Ambaula kabotu.
    Talk properly.

14. Luyaba: Ya, **very good**, kutali mbooli kwaambaula ccita oko. Kkala waambaule.
    Yes, very good, not the way you were talking [before]. Sit here and talk.

[Gary bends his forehead towards Luyaba and sticks his fingers out from his forehead, pretending to bellow at her like a bull.]

15. Gary: Moo! Moo!
    Moo! Moo!

16. Emma [to the others]: Atucuume bbwe kusyule.
    Let's beat her [Luyaba] with a stone at the back.

17. Luyaba [to Emma, scared]: Ka, Mama kaka mulandi ... Naa tamuyandi ...
    Ka, Mama, please, you'll ... If you don't want ...

18. Emma [to Luyaba, sternly]: Teki kaka, ulimupati.
    Teki please, you're [too] old [to be scared by a game like this].

[Gary and now Brian pretend to be bulls attacking Luyaba.]

19. Luyaba: Ndaleka buyo kusobana.
    I'll stop playing the game.

20. Emma: Kuli wasula.
    Someone farted.

21. Luyaba [laughing]: Mebo ndinvwide kununkilila.
    To me, it's a good smell.

22. Emma [pointing at Brian]: Nceeci awa [casula].

   It's this one [who farted].

23. Luyaba: Yebo Brian.

   You, Brian.

[Brian laughs. Emma whispers something inaudible to Luyaba.]

24. Luyaba [to Emma]: Kamuumuna buyo, mwanvwa? Not kufwubaazyanya, kwiina bubi.

   Keep quiet, okay? Don't rebuke your friends. It's not a problem if they do that.

As the oldest girl present in the group above, Luyaba is likely to be held responsible for anything occurring while the adults are away, and so she adopts the role of primary caretaker and authority, surveilling, assessing and moderating everyone's actions against general behavioural norms. When her 3-year-old cousin John jokingly challenges her authority by telling her she is 'foolish' (*yanga-yanga*, line 11), she reminds him how 'that's not the way you [should] talk, talk properly' (lines 12), and when he acknowledges her correction she responds 'Yes, *very good*' (line 14), using an English, teacher-like expression to assert her authority. While thus positioning herself through powerful discourse, Luyaba still seeks the companionship of her younger peers, openly criticising her aunt Clarence's distribution of sugarcane and subsequent accusation of theft with her younger sister Emma (lines 3, 5), joking with her young cousin John (lines 7–8) and tentatively joining in with her cousins Gary and Brian's role play of attacking bull (lines 15–17). 6-year-old Emma challenges her older sister Luyaba's authority, reproving their cousin John for overeating (line 1) and Brian for farting (line 22), while telling Luyaba she is 'too old' (*ulimupati*) to engage emotionally in her cousins' silly game (line 18). Interestingly, Emma does not accuse her 9-year-old cousin Brian of being 'too old' to play bullfight although he is the same age as Luyaba. This could be read as a gendered distinction, drawing on adults' general application of larger social responsibility and earlier maturity to girls than boys. At the age of nine, Luyaba is starting to be regarded as a young woman (*mukaintu*) in local society, in being ascribed increasing chores and responsibilities along with certain powers over her younger peers. Luyaba accepts Emma's accusation and announces her departure of the game (line 19). As 6-year-old Emma goes on to accuse Brian of farting, Luyaba rebukes her, telling her to stop rebuking the others for trivial matters (line 24).

In Hang'ombe, adults mostly left children to solve conflicts on their own, encouraging older children to be stern on younger peers. I sometimes overheard children telling peers 'I am old' (*ndimupati*), legitimising their attainment of a particularly nice dress, toy or piece of meat, but children's power negotiations often occurred through more sophisticated discursive means, especially by the age of six or seven as their language skills improved. As another example of this, I observed five children from the Mweemba *munzi* hanging out in the grassfields one Sunday morning in May 2009, including 9-year-old Luyaba and her cousin Brian (9), who appeared above, along with Luyaba's brothers Daala (9) and Edson (6) and Brian's younger brother Gary (5). The four boys were in charge of herding the cattle, while Luyaba had joined them for a few hours, escaping her cooking chores. For a while, the children played several rounds of the popular game *kupwa*,[2] throwing and catching a small rock in the air with one hand while removing other rocks from a small hole in the ground with the other. At one point, Edson became upset from just having lost another round of kupwa to his cousin Brian. He kicked Brian's collection of stones and scattered them around, leading Brian to call him *'Bausyi Dumbo'* ('Dumbo's grandfather'), a common nickname associated with being fat or stupid, originating from Walt Disney's classical film version of Helen Aberson's book *Dumbo: The Flying Elephant*, which had been screened several times on the chiTonga entertainment programme *Kantuunya Kamu Nsabata* (*The Saturday Play*). This nickname roused the laughter of the other children, infuriating Edson even more:[3]

1. Brian [to Edson]: Bausyi Dumbo!

    Dumbo's grandfather!

    [The other children laugh. Edson is upset and starts beating both Daala and Brian.]

2. Daala [laughing, to Edson]: Koya uume wakwiita kuti 'Bausyi Dumbo' utaumi ndime.

    Go beat the one calling you 'Bausyi Dumbo', don't beat me.

3. Daala [to all]: Ndaleka kusobana Edson tacizyi kusobana.

    I have stopped playing because Edson doesn't know how to play.

    [Edson is infuriated by this and continues to punch both Daala and Brian.]

4. Daala [to Edson, angrily]: Nseyandi yawe. Edson nhi! Nhi!
      I don't want you [to do this]. Edson, no! No!

5. Gary [laughing]: Edson tacizyi kusobana …
      Edson doesn't know how to play …

6. Brian [to Edson]: Hei! Edson …
      Hey! Edson …

   [Edson screams, while beating both Brian and Gary.]

7. Gary [to Edson, jokingly]: Yebo cinya cako …
      You piece of shit …

8. Daala [to Gary, jokingly]: Mbomutukana nkomuzwa?
      Is that how you insult in your house?

   [The children laugh at Daala's remark. Brian starts beating Edson back.]

9. Daala [to Brian and Edson]: Kwiina kulwana, kamwaambaula buyo.
      You shouldn't fight, just speak.

10. Luyaba [agreeing with this]: Tukkopwa buya.
      We are being recorded.

   [Some seconds pass. Edson stops beating Brian and sits by himself
   for a while. Brian and Daala begin writing with sticks on the ground in
   front of the children, using humorously exaggerated movements.]

11. Brian [to the others]: Sena wabona bwakulemba?
      Have you seen how we write?

12. Daala [holding a stick]: Basa ndiyanda kulemba zyina lya chiDumbo.
      Friends, I want to write the name chiDumbo ['the Dumbo'].

   [Edson remains seated but is upset by the writing. Gary and Luyaba are
   laughing, while Daala and Brian keep writing in the sand.]

13. Edson [angrily, to Daala]: Ndamuuma umwi!
      I will beat you!

14. Daala [while writing in the sand]: *Ngooyu 'Dumbo'.*
      Here is [the name] 'Dumbo'.

15. Edson [to Daala, angrily]: Fuseke!
      Go away!

   [Edson is about to cry and runs off, while Daala and Brian continue
   writing with sticks in the sand.]

This interaction circles around the mocking of 6-year-old Edson lead by Daala (9) and Brian (9), supported by the laughter and cheering of Luyaba (9) and Gary (5). Edson tries to challenge the two older boys by beating and screaming, but he fails and eventually runs off crying. Instead of retaliating, Daala maintains power as both commander of international media discourse – repeating the nickname *Bausyi Dumbo* (line 2) – and as moral authority, telling the others how 'Edson doesn't know how to play' (line 3). An adult might criticise a loud or impudent child for not knowing how to play, criticising his or her lack of social adaptability and responsibility, which was considered a grave charge. Daala thus positions himself as a knowledgeable and mature person, who, unlike Edson, does not need to use violence to assert himself. The same pattern is visible in Daala's later reproof of Brian and Edson, 'You shouldn't fight, just speak' (line 9). Both attempts seem to enhance Daala's moral authority among his peers, who laugh and cheer while supporting his authoritative approach, like Luyaba telling the others 'We are being recorded' (line 10). Imitating adults' moral discourse thus served as an efficient social strategy especially among older children, maintaining and enhancing their recognition among peers. Contrary to much adult talk, however, children's power negotiations were often humorous and excessive, creating amusing insults and mocking the dramatic voices and registers of local authorities. This appears in 5-year-old Gary calling Edson 'You piece of shit' (line 7) and Daala's subsequent rebuke, 'Is that how you insult in your house' (line 8), both delivered with overly dramatic voices that evoke the enthused laughter of their bystanding peers. I once watched a group of 5- and 6-year-old girls calling each other *mazi aankuku yaba taata* ('You shit of my father's hen') over and over while falling into fits of laughter. This practice of turning prohibited language into powerful means of entertainment and self-assertion has been observed in other studies of children's peer talk. Drawing on linguistic-anthropological studies of *ritual insults* among underprivileged, young Black male Americans in the 1970s (Abrahams 1974; Kochman 1983; Labov 1972), language socialisation scholar Ann-Carita Evaldsson describes how a group of Swedish school boys with immigrant – and thus socially marginalised – backgrounds used humorous and inventive insults to establish and reorganise powerful, masculine identities for themselves (Evaldsson 2005). She notes how '… a variety of negative descriptions are mobilized in the process of insulting, making relevant and reorganising local norms of conduct, membership categories and institutional frameworks' (Evaldsson 2005: 783). This analysis may also be applied to Hang'ombe boys and girls, intermediately reorganising and subverting prevailing hierarchies through their playful exaggeration and mocking of local authorities.

Children's power acquisition among peers thus relied not only on the mastery of adult discourse but also on the courage and means to challenge it. This appears in the last part of the extract above as Daala and Brian start making letter-like symbols with sticks in the sand while announcing, 'Have you seen how we write?' (line 11), 'Friends, I want to write the name 'chiDumbo'' (line 12) and 'Here is the name *Dumbo*' (line 14), still using mocking voices and exaggerated gestures. Although the boys' actual writing skills might be sparse, this appears to infuriate and humiliate Edson even more, now seeing his nickname outlined and 'formalised' on the ground. Observing people around them, the children learned how the display of formal education like writing, counting and the use of English terms earnt them recognition and respect; for example, from their older siblings in higher grades. As I illustrate in Chapter 4, children often used school-associated practices to assert themselves, but they could also be heard mocking the chanting speech of teachers or their proud display of academic skills. In the extract above, the fact that Daala and Brian, unlike Edson, had both started school was likely to enhance their position, allowing them to both imitate and mock teachers and thus establish themselves as knowledgeable authorities among their peers.

Negotiating Family Hierarchies

A special role in many local households pertained to children spending shorter or longer periods with extended family members in Hang'ombe, mostly because their parents were either deceased or had moved away for work or remarriage and/or found themselves physically and financially incapable of taking care of one or more of their children and had thus decided to place them in the care of extended relatives. These children were referred to as 'dependants' (*mulelwa*) and often assumed a more subdued position in family hierarchies than children living with one or both their parents. Some dependants were known to be given larger or more strenuous chores than their cousins living within the same household – even if they were of the same age and gender – just as some dependants were allegedly given less food and basic commodities like clothes, shoes, pens and notebooks than their peers. Among the families I observed, however, such distinction or discrimination seemed to figure primarily in adults' attempts to tell me and each other what kind of family and caretakers they were *not* – that is, uneducated and 'backwards' (*budalu*), instead positioning themselves as good Christians who treated all their children fairly and equally. The six 'dependant' children I came to know in Hang'ombe – 10-year-old Frida and 9-year-old Richwel, living with their relatives in the Mweemba homestead; 11-year-old Malilwe and her sister Shimbi (6), living with their grandparents and thirteen other extended family members in the Phiri homestead; and 13-year-old Mutinta and her 6-year-old sister old Senefa, living with their five cousins, their aunt and grandparents in the Hang'ombe homestead – all seemed to maintain chores and privileges quite similar to those of their 'parented' cousins. However, I did observe such affinity-based discrimination produced among children themselves, reactivating available categories and distinctions in order to advance their own social position against their peers.

The extract below was recorded on a Wednesday afternoon in October 2008, when 11-year-old Malilwe was walking home from school with her two young uncles Solomon (9) and Julu (11), all living in the same household of the Phiri munzi with Malilwe's sister Shimbi (6) and the boys' four other siblings – Clever (6), Miyoba (7), Brenda (9) and Mwiinga (15) – and their parents (Malilwe and Shimbi's grandparents) Shadrik and Love. About one year prior, Malilwe's mother Prudence had asked her mother Love to take care of Malilwe and Shimbi, since Prudence had remarried a man who did not want the girls to stay in his home, most likely because he did not want to feed or have expenses for more children. Malilwe and Shimbi had thus come to stay in the Phiri munzi in late 2007, assisting their grandmother in the housekeeping and going to the local school with her aunts and uncles. As the three children walked along the path, Malilwe urged Julu and Solomon to defend her against her two aunts Miyoba (7) and Brenda (9) – Julu and Solomon's sisters – who Malilwe feared might exploit her vulnerable position as a dependant by imposing their cooking chores on her. As the extract begins, Malilwe reminds Julu and Solomon of how her grandmother Love told her daughters Miyoba and Brenda earlier that same day that they were 'old enough' (*bapati-pati*) to prepare today's evening meal themselves, thus releasing Malilwe from her usual responsibility. Malilwe then goes on to defend her grandmother against other family members' charges against her for mistreating another dependant child, 9-year-old Tengi, who stayed with Love and her family about a year ago when her mother Roleen – Love's younger sister – found it difficult to provide for her children herself. This arrangement caused conflict between Roleen and Love, evoking issues of child-rearing and personal moral:

1. Malilwe [to Julu and Solomon]: Nobantu, ede mwalinvwide nibaamba kuti Miyoba a Brenda bakatwe musozya?

   People, did you hear when she [Love] said Miyoba and Brenda should prepare sampa?

2. Julu: liyi.

   Yes.

3. Malilwe: Mukandibede bakamboni, mbobacita. Balo baakusika ulanvwa baambila nduwe kuti tutwe toonse. Ede bataambe kuti 'Malilwe ukatwe musozya'? Mpoonya bazyooamba kuti 'bakatwe buyo Miyoba a Brenda bapati-pati'.

   You should be my witness to what they [Miyoba and Brenda] do. When we arrive home they'll tell me to prepare the sampa. Do you remember she [Love] said 'Malilwe you should prepare sampa'? Then she changed and said 'Brenda and Miyoba who are old enough should prepare the sampa'.

4. Julu and Solomon: liyi.

   Yes.

[The children walk quietly for a while.]

5. Malilwe: Tengi ukkede kabotu nkwakkede oko. At ncitwe buyo kwiina maanu.

   Tengi is okay where she is now. She [Love] used to say that Tengi has no manners.

6. Julu: Nguni wakaammba?

   Who said that?

7. Malilwe: Ati Tengi wakonzya banyina. Ati ndaaye nibakaakusika ku Mandala kuya, mbobakali kwaamba, ati nibakabuzya kuti ino yawe mwana oyu wakajoka buti, balo balaamba koo Muleya bana tiibakali kulya kabotu. Wabona Tengi bakamwiima bread njobakaula bausyi. Buzuba Tengi mbobakalileta bread, banene balaamba ba Tengi kamutwaabanya ndinwe mulaabauso batupa bread. Tengi wakaamba kuti peepe, mpoonya bakagusya tu license [slices] tobilo bapa bahaanene. Komwe balya ka license [slices].

   She [Love] said Tengi took after her mother. When she [Roleen] arrived at Mandala, when she [Roleen] was asked the reason why Tengi stopped staying with Love, she said that the child [Tengi] was not kept well by Love. She also said that Tengi was not given the bread [by Love] that her father bought for her. The day the bread was brought, my grandmother [Love] told Tengi to share us the bread. Tengi refused to share, but then

> *Love got two licenses [slices] and gave them to my grandfather [Shadrik]. Love ate one license [slice].*

8. Solomon [laughing]: Tu 'licence'?

   You're saying 'licence'?

9. Malilwe: Toonse otu ubape beenzyinyoko, mpoonya watupa two, two, two mpoonya walo walya totatwe. Mpoonya sugar balaamba ba Tengi kamuliyobola ndinwe mulaabauso. Mpoonya Tengi ulaamba katulibikka buyo mubwatu lyoonse sugar eli mucigomo. Mpoonya walo naakamana nkuyooambila banyina kuti bakandiima bread. Mpoonya naakamana mazuba banene baakuula bread bamupa Tengi balaamba 'eli nde bread ndyobakakuulila bauso'.

   > *Tengi was told to share the rest [of the slices] among us, then she [Tengi] gave us two, two, two [slices] each, then she ate three. Then Love told Tengi to keep the sugar because she is the owner of the father who bought it. Then Tengi suggested that the sugar be put in the pot of sweet beer. Then Tengi went and told her mother 'they ate all my bread'. After some days my grandmother bought bread and gave it to Tengi and said 'here is the bread your father bought you'.*

[Julu and Solomon do not respond. The children remain quiet for awhile after this.]

Rather than complaining to her grandmother, who is unlikely to intervene in the children's conflict anyway, Malilwe aligns herself with her young uncles, in this case by reminding them of Love's instructions earlier that day (lines 1–4). With this alignment in place, Malilwe meticulously retells some incidents of significance in relation to the current dispute between Love and her sister Roleen on the matter of Roleen's daughter (and Malilwe's cousin) Tengi, who – like Malilwe – had stayed in Love's care one year before, together with Malilwe. Early on during Tengi's stay, her father Chilima had apparently bought some bread and sugar for Tengi to eat. According to Malilwe's recount, Love told Tengi to share the bread between herself and her extended family members, which Tengi 'refused', leading Love to take two bread slices for herself and her husband Shadrik (line 7) and force Tengi to share the rest of the bread between herself and her cousins. Later on, Tengi allegedly told her mother how the family 'ate all my bread' (line 9) – concealing significant details of her herself eating three slides and getting to keep the sugar for herself – thus presenting Love and her family members as greedy and ill-mannered. When Love got hold of this account, she apparently bought Tengi new bread and told her 'here is the bread your father bought you', thus disclaiming both Tengi and her parents' accusations against her (line 9). The extract above reveals 11-year-old Malilwe's close understanding of family relationships and the strife of food allocation in a society marked by periodical scarcity. Aligning herself with her two cousins through moral discourse, reproducing details of speech and action in the compounding of distinct but thematically related events, she seeks to enhance her vulnerable position in the family hierarchy. Julu and Solomon may not fully grasp the social implications of this report, including its relevance for Malilwe's previous attempt at justifying herself against her aunts Miyoba and Brenda's harassments by reminding Julu and Solomon of their mother Love's favourable distribution of cooking chores earlier that day (lines 1–4). But by practising and extending her discursive skills, Malilwe may gradually enhance her vulnerable position among her peers and extended family members.

Decoding Delicate Knowledge

As noted before, adults rarely sat down and talked elaborately with children until they were considered young adults themselves – that is, around the age of 12–13.[4] Until then, children acquired most social knowledge through their peers and by observing and eavesdropping on adults during work, meals and nightly fires at home or while passing through the township and marketplace on their way to or from school. The relatively free exposure to adults' everyday talk and activities provided children with insights into grave concerns like family conflicts or marital problems, the sickness of a family member, political tension or the prospects of hunger during periods of drought. Children often shared such delicate knowledge with peers, impressing each other and trying to make sense of it all without much assistance from adults. This was also the case one early February morning, when 11-year-old Malilwe and her two maternal aunts, 7-year-old Miyoba and 9-year-old Brenda, walked from the Phiri homestead towards the garden about 3 km away to assist their grandmother and mother Love in the weeding of vegetables. The three girls were walking on their own, Malilwe holding the recorder. Meanwhile, they shared their impressions of a vehement argument occurring the previous night between Love's 20-year-old nephew Obrian and his wife Sarah or *bina Junior*, who shared a separate house in the girls' homestead together with their 6-month-old son Junior:

1. Malilwe: Jilo ba uncle bakabatanda bina Junior, bakalwana badaala. Nkiinga Junior kulila. Mane beenda amasiku. Ndakanvwa buyo bantu bapanga coongo ani balalwana. Ba uncle bakali koledwe.

   > Yesterday uncle [Obrian] chased bina Junior, they were fighting. Junior cried. She went away in the night. I heard the noise from the people. I didn't know they were fighting. My uncle was drunk.

2. Brenda: Kayi bina Junior bakatukana ba uncle nibakasika balikoledwe.

   > Mother of Junior insulted uncle who was drunk.

3. Miyoba: Nkaambo bamulamu balatukana, mane balaamba ati 'omubwa'. Nkujana baama banyamuka bainka.

   > My sister-in-law insults [a lot], she said 'you dog'. My mother stood up and went [over there].

4. Brenda: Ino bakalila bina Junior.

   > Bina Junior cried.

5. Malilwe: Bakamutola amwana [sena]?

   > Did she go with the child [Junior]?

6. Miyoba: Mwana wacaala a Mwiinga. Mbuli kuti ba Obrian bafwumina kwa Nebon ancinga.

   > The child remained with Mwiinga. It seems Obrian has gone to Nebon's home on a bike.

[After this, the girls remain quiet for a while, whereafter they begin to discuss other topics.]

Malilwe, Brenda and Miyoba all seem to have captured parts of the argument and the subsequent departure of bina Junior to her father Nebon's homestead a few kilometres away, leaving her baby Junior behind with the girls' older sister/aunt, 15-year-old Mwiinga. This event evoked prevailing norms of gender, marriage and kinship, along with the social repercussions of alcohol abuse and the vulnerability of especially young women in marital conflict, often compelling them to leave their husband's home and seek refuge with their own parents while leaving their children behind. At their relatively young age, the three girls above may not understand all the social implications of the previous night's events, but by sharing and discussing their observations among each other they might reach a satisfying joint interpretation, helping them prepare themselves for their own potential futures as wives and mothers in local society. Like in earlier examples, the girls above seek to assert themselves in the group by drawing on powerful moral discourse, like Malilwe and Brenda both implicitly blaming Obrian for being drunk (lines 1 and 2), and Brenda and Miyoba both mentioning how Sarah or bina Junior insulted her husband by calling him *omubwa* or 'you dog' and is known to 'insult a lot' (lines 2 and 3). As I discussed in Chapter 2, women were more likely than men to be denoted as bunkanwe or 'gossipy', a highly derogatory term associated with being lazy, defiant and sexually loose. On the other hand, alcohol abuse was considered an equally immoral practice in local society. By construing the previous night's events as caused by the encounter of Obrian's alleged alcohol abuse and bina Junior's gossipy personality, Malilwe, Brenda and Miyoba together manage both to mitigate a potentially frightening experience and to assert themselves as mature and morally righteous. As we have seen, Hang'ombe children's peer interactions thus posed as a central arena for their exploration and acquisition of significant cultural knowledge, including delicate issues rarely discussed between children and adults. Adults sometimes capitalised on children's relative freedom of movement and access to delicate knowledge, interrogating them about other people's behaviours and even directing them to pursue particular issues for them. In the brief extract below recorded in the Phiri homestead one evening in March 2009, only a few weeks after the dramatic event depicted above, 18-year-old Sarah thus questioned her husband Obrian's nephews, 9-year-old Solomon and 11-year-old Julu, on the relationship status of a local young villager named Tom, whose younger brothers often spent time with Solomon and Julu in the cattle fields:

1. Sarah [to Solomon]: Ino Tom ulisyabide?
   Is Tom in a relationship?

2. Julu: Kuli yuulya kayi?
   With that one?

3. Sarah: Enhe?
   Yes?

4. Julu: Nkwalala kayi.
   That is where he sleeps.

5. Sarah [to Solomon]: Tom nkwalala?
   Does Tom sleep [at her house]?

6. Solomon: Iiyi.
   Yes.

The children I observed seemed somewhat uncomfortable around such pushed disclosure to parents or other adults, accentuating their low family status and perhaps forcing them to report on friends and their family members and touch upon delicate issues like alcohol abuse, marital conflict or romance, like above. To me, such incidents seemed to disrupt children's experience of being left to roam around and explore largely uninhibited, reminding them of this freedom being subject to parental control.

Mocking Authority in Role Play

As we have seen, children often used moral discourse to obtain and maintain authority among peers, lecturing each other about the calamities of idleness, bad hygiene, badmouthing and parental disobedience, or negotiating proper conduct during games and fights while at the same time testing and mocking such discourse. This occurred both during serious and more playful interactions among peers, but a particularly dense display of children's mockery of moral discourse happened during their activities of role or sociodramatic play. In Hang'ombe, such activities were most prominent among girls and often evoked scenarios associated with the household, like mother and daughter(s) or mother and (female) friend(s), but they might also draw on other arenas, like teacher and student(s), doctor and patient(s) or preacher and worshipper(s), visible both among girls and boys. In line with language socialisation scholars' observations of children in various Western and majority settings (De León 2007; Goodwin and Kyratzis 2012; Kyratzis 2007; Paugh 2005; Reynolds 2013; Rindstedt 2001), activities of pretend play enabled Hang'ombe children to enact and mock the solemn speech of authoritative figures controlling them and their social environments in daily life, often using humorous and highly creative discursive means. As an example, the following extract was recorded in the Hang'ombe homestead one afternoon in May 2009 during the month-long school break marking the final part of the harvesting season. 8-year-old Lushomo and her 6-year-old cousin Senefa were playing in their mutual 'play field' (*cibuwa cakusobanina*), a small piece of dried-up land designated by families for the play and early farming practice of young children. The girls had been busy helping Lushomo's mother Minivah with the peeling of maize and had now been dismissed for the afternoon, on condition that they took along Lushomo's baby sister Lweendo, now hanging on Senefa's back. Although the soil was arid and had not produced crops for long, the girls were eagerly hacking with small sticks in the ground, pretending to be searching for and digging up sweet potatoes like they had seen their mothers and older siblings do many times in the fields around them. After a while, Lushomo's 3-year-old brother Habeenzu joined in, grapping a stick and trying to keep up with the girls' conversation, which had now moved on to other aspects of farming, like the risk of enraging dangerous insects if hitting a wrong spot with one's hoe, and the general hardships of manual labour. Gradually, without explicit coordination, the children's conversation evolved into a family role play, with Lushomo taking the self-designated role of the mother, and Senefa and Habeenzu acting as her (teenage) daughter and son. Lushomo acted rather bossily, ordering her peers to 'dig harder into the ground' (*kusyisya*) and warning Senefa against 'dropping the child' (*kuunsya mwana*), still sitting on her back. At one point, when Habeenzu had drifted off to dig by himself, Lushomo brought up the issue of 'boyfriends' (*basankwa*), accusing Senefa in a humorously high-pitched voice and dramatic gestures of 'moving with boys' (*kweenda aankako*) – that is, secretly experimenting with sex and romance:[5]

1. Lushomo [to Senefa, sternly]: Mamii mo!
    Hey, Mama!

2. Senefa: Hee?
    What?

3. Lushomo [in low voice]: Ntwaanzi tusankwa ntomweeteeta?
    What do you do with the boys you bring?

4. Senefa [hesitant]: Kwiina …
    Nothing …

5. Lushomo [in low voice]: Mbuyanga mani. 'Kwiina' kuli? …
    Ndiyookuuma kuti nkakujane aaka sankwa … Nkaakaya kana Sinambili.
    Mwaali kweenda aankako.
    You fool. 'Nothing', you say? … I will beat you if I find you with that boy. It is that boy from Sinambili [Village]. You were moving with him.

6. Senefa [insecure]: Peepe. Naamulayanda mumubuzye Habeenzu.
    Nseendi aanguwe.
    No. If you want, you can ask Habeenzu. I don't go out with him.

7. Lushomo [sternly]: Zyakuubiila yana kumulu ccindi mubuzyizye nzi! …
Koti ndilamubuzye asika.

>   *I will beat you, you are lying! … I will ask him when he comes
>   back.*

8. Senefa [hesitant]: Niini oyo … niini oyo …

>   *This one … this one … [trying to remember a boy's name].*

9. Lushomo: Borne? [the name of a boy who recently visited from
another *village*].

>   *Borne?*

10. Senefa [low voice]: Borne. Wainkide kokuya.

>   *Borne. He went [back] there [to his village].*

11. Lushomo: Ndamubuzya buya. Kuti 'Weenda aani? Weenda aani?'
Ndamubuzya kuti 'Weendaani?' Ndamubuzya. Beenzyinyoko
balandaambila kuti inga ulilide kucikolo nainga mali. Waajana kuli?

>   *I will ask him [Habeenzu]. I'll say, 'Who does she move with?
>   Who does she move with?' I'll ask him 'Who does she move
>   with?' I will ask him. Your friends tell me that you eat a lot at
>   school. Where do you get the money?*

[Senefa does not respond. Lushomo turns to Habeenzu, who is playing
on the grass nearby.]

12. Lushomo: Habeenzu!

>   *Habeenzu!*

13. Habeenzu: Hee?

>   *What?*

14. Lushomo: Oyu weendaani oyu?

>   *Who does this one [Senefa] move with?*

15. Habeenzu: Hee?

>   *What?*

16. Lushomo: Oyu, Mama. Wendaani? Musankwa wakwe? Huh?

>   *This one, Mama. Who does she move with? Who is her
>   boyfriend? Huh?*

17. Habeenzu [low voice]: Ccita.

>   *I don't know.*

18. Lushomo [to Habeenzu]: Akaya ndakabona kaya!

>   *I saw her and you with that boy!*

19. Lushomo [to Senefa, sternly]: Mwakali kweenda eliya buzuba ankako.
Ati naa, nda ... ati ati ... ati ncomunga, ati ncomunga, ati ncomunga
nywe mulakaka-kaka kakwiita kasankwa ... ati tamukaki, umwi one day
kazyoomutolela limwi. Nciindi cenu we kamweebelezya.

> You were moving [with him] that day. This manner ... I ... this
> this ... this manner in which ... this manner in which you don't
> say no to calls from boys ... this ... one day he will take you [with
> him]. That is your own fault.

[The girls remain quiet for a while after this, still working in the play
field.]

Among Hang'ombe families, I frequently overheard mothers
scolding their teenage daughters in a register similar to the one
adopted by 8-year-old Lushomo above, using subtle metaphors for
sexual conduct like 'bringing boys' (line 3), 'moving with boys' (line
5), 'eating a lot' (line 11) – that is, receiving food, money and other
gifts from alleged lovers – and 'not saying no to calls from boys' (line
19). However, by adopting a humorously exaggerated high-pitched
voice and dramatic gestures, Lushomo seems to aim for a different
purpose than the mere reprimand of her (fictitious) young daughter.
Rather, she might be performing for a wider audience, like me and
Khama, sitting about 15 metres away, displaying a humorous and
somewhat controversial ability to mock overzealous mothers. While
on one hand Lushomo reproduces common negative stereotypes of
young women's promiscuity and moral weakness, she simultaneously
mocks and criticises the moral assumptions embedded in such
stereotypes. Senefa seems less comfortable than Lushomo with the
role she has been assigned, responding hesitantly to her 'mother's'
threats and accusations, the implicit meaning of which she may not
fully understand. Still, Senefa tries to defend herself, denying the
charges (line 4), aligning herself with young Habeenzu (line 6) and
suggesting that a boy named Borne, who recently visited the girls'
homestead from a neighbouring village, has now 'gone back there'
(line 10). In her young age, 6-year-old Senefa thus already shows some
awareness of the moral codices commonly ascribed to young women
in the region, of virtuousness, chastity and obedience – codices that
she complies with and thus reproduces above. In line with Ann-Carita
Evaldsson's observation of ethnic minority boys' use of *ritual insults*
in a Swedish school (Evaldsson 2005), my thesis is that – like adults –
Hang'ombe children generally sought to understand and appropriate
existing power structures, utilising them whenever they sustained
their position favourably but also challenging them if the situation

allowed and called for it. As they grew into young women, girls like Lushomo were likely to be increasingly subjected to existing norms of gender, age and kinship relations, but their subtle rebellion against local hierarchies might indicate impending social change.

Children were exposed to another, more institutionalised kind of authority with weekly Adventist sermons, where preachers spoke in loud, solemn voices, reminding the congregation of the importance of serving God and following the prescriptions of the Bible. Preachers were broadly admired and respected, and extracts of a particularly striking sermon were sometimes repeated and discussed during family gatherings at night. I often heard children using expressions like 'God will punish you' (*mwami ulamuuma*) when rebuking toddlers, or calling each other a 'dirty sinner' when, for example, fighting about whether or not someone had been cheating during play. School-aged children might evoke the impending arrival of 'the last day' and the importance of remaining 'good in the eyes of God' in order to 'reach Heaven', thus recalling common church discourse. On several occasions, I observed children – both boys and girls – mocking the thundering rebukes of an angry preacher in front of their peers, imitating his fierce voice and dramatic gestures and making him into a somewhat ridiculous but also very impressive character. One example of this occurred one morning in February 2009, when 7-year- old Miyoba was sitting with her 6-month-old cousin Junior on a mat on the floor in the cikuta or visitors' hall in the Phiri homestead. Her mother and older sisters were preparing supper in the kitchen hall about 20 metres away, and she had accepted my placement of the digital recorder next to her – but apart from that, Miyoba seemed to be joking and performing mainly for the sake of her own entertainment. As the extract below begins, she is trying to give Junior a lukewarm cup of tea, playfully rebuking him for pushing the tea away:

1. Miyoba: Yoonse eyi njootila yalinji awa njootila. Nkooko. Nceeci cikapu we nauyanda kuti ndicite buti nsyii! … Nsyi, nsyi, nsyi, hehehe! [laughing demonstratively]. Ci tea camana, yawe cana. Mboopya utalike kulila … Kutegwa upye?

   > *There is no more [tea], look. Take it [the cup]. You have poured down a lot of tea, that's okay! … Take it, take it, take it, hehehe! [laughing demonstratively]. The tea has finished, you bad baby. She has burnt herself … You start crying now?*

2. [sternly]: Yebo. Mpotikkale awa utete tubone utete unywaame. Unywaame. Mpoyanda kulala awa abbuda. Walitesya caali.

You. This is where you will have to sit [on the wet mat]. I want you to get soaked. You get soaked. We shall sit on this wet mat. You made it wet on purpose.

[Miyoba whisks away the flies that have been attracted by the spilled tea.]

3. [screaming]: Nzinini azyalo zyatalika!

   The flies have come!

4. [screaming]: **He! Hey! Hey! Hey! What about this? Huh?**

   Hi! Hey! Hey! Hey! What about this? Huh?

[Mimicking English-like sounds in dramatic tone.]

5. [loudly]: Hamashmlamshla mshla brrrrrrrlllsbrrrr hahe! Una!

   Together! From here. In one poem I take all the people had ... had minee!

   Hamashmlamshla mshla brrrrrrrlllsbrrrr hahe! Oops! Together! From here. In one poem I take all the people had ... had mine!

6. ['preaching']: Bomboyamba? Caamba kuti, 'kokkalikila mwana yebo!' Ulyanzi kale? Matwi ayo. Kunoopailila. Zikinya matwi. Azyoomugali-gali. Azyoomugali-gali mutwe so. Kuzyoo mujwa! Kumujwa nyemu mumutwe. Ulanditonka. Unditonkelanzi?

   Are you listening? That means, 'behave, you baby'! Are you eating again? I will pray for you. I will shake your ears. Shaking the ears, shaking the ears like this. Pulling them out. You are pushing me! Why are you pushing me?

[Miyoba gently pulls Lweendo's ears, then lets her go as she starts singing.]

7. [singing]: Pele bulowa bwa Jeesu.

   Only the blood of Jesus.

8. ['preaching']: Zyimane zyibi zyako zyili mumutwe omo. Zyimane zyoonse tukupailile. Yebo mwana yebo. Nzinini zyandisyupa! So, musaangune kundipailila, mebo. Mutaangune yooyu uugalangene, uusyupide kulila koonse-koonse-koonse.

   All the sins in your head shall finish. All the sins in you will finish when we pray for you. The flies are annoying me, so you should pray for me! But first, pray for this one [Lweendo] who is ugly and crying-crying-crying.

9. [screaming, in English]: **And my skirt!!! Huh! Has a people if he can't me!! ... Has a people, people together! I want to gather my meee ...**

> *And my skirt!!! Huh! Has a people if he can't me!! … Has a*
> *people, people together! I want to gather my meee …*

10. [singing]: **My talk to meee, my follow people, my churchie, my daddyni, my follow people … Huti meeeeee! Huti can't me … by talking! For the poem! For the poem titled** 'Tola, mutolo, mutolo tayelede kulya pe'.

> *My talk to meee, my follow people, my churchie, my daddyni,*
> *my follow people … Huti meeeeee! Huti can't me … by*
> *talking! For the poem! For the poem titled 'Lazy, a lazy, lazy*
> *person should not eat'.*

11. [yelling]: Yebo! Nhi! nhi! nhi! nhi! Mutolo, oyu mwana mutolo, mutolo oyu mwana tuyanda kuti abe muyumu. Abe muyumu tumukambaukile, tubaite bapasita bamuka. Yebo, yebo, yebo, yebo.

> *You! My, my, my, my! This baby is lazy. This baby is lazy, now we*
> *want him to be strong. He should be strong so we shall preach*
> *to him. We shall call the pastor to preach for him. You, you,*
> *you.*

[Miyoba continues like this for several minutes.]

7-year-old Miyoba here employs a number of performative features characteristic of sermons in the local Adventist church, especially identifiable in her use of an oratorical voice, shifting between whispering, chanting, screaming and singing. She also evokes several linguistic features common to preachers, code-switching back and forth between English and chiTonga (lines 10, 12), using rhetorical questions like 'Are you listening?' (line 6), desires of wanting 'to pray for this one who is ugly and crying' (line 8) and other religious expressions, like 'the blood of Jesus' (line 7) 'finishing the sins in your head' (line 8), 'a people together!' (line 9) and 'my follow people' (line 10), both in chiTonga and English. As a second grader, Miyoba has only recently been introduced to English at school, and she has not mastered more than a few English phrases and fixed expressions. This is visible, for example, in her gibberish expressions, like 'In one poem I take all the people had … had minee!' (line 5) and 'Has a people if he can't me!' (line 9), uttered in a dramatic voice. But in spite of her limited proficiency, Miyoba has clearly realised the performative value of the English language in a community associating it with the school, the clinic, the city and the West (Spitulnik 1998). Adopting an advanced register commonly associated with preachers, including a solemn voice, dramatic gestures and rhetorical rebukes against little baby Junior, Miyoba turns the discourse of a formal, authoritative figure like the preacher into a quite impressive but also ridiculing performance. Creatively mixing roles and registers, she combines her preacher-like character with the role of an angry parent, scolding her baby sister for spilling tea all over the floor (line 1). This parent is subject to an equal dramatisation, using sarcasm like 'You start crying now?' (line 1), pejoratives like 'bad child' (line 1), 'ugly' (line 8) and 'lazy' (line 11), and threats like 'I want you to get soaked' and 'we shall sit on this wet mat' (line 2). In line with the previous interactions, I perceive Miyoba's performance as a simultaneous attempt to explore and position herself towards a particular social order prevailing around her. Exhibiting the contradictory nature of the authoritative discourse employed by adult figures around her, she asserts herself as a competent and self-assured family and community member.

Conclusion

With their peers, Hang'ombe children processed the delicate social information exposed to them in daily village life, like parental ambiguities, fluctuating family hierarchies, marital conflicts, the moral education of young girls or the contradictions of religious doctrine. Through skilful observation and eavesdropping, they learned how particular social rules applied to some situations and not others and how they might enhance themselves in the fragile hierarchies of local homesteads. While playing or working together on their own, they tried out different adult roles and registers, scolding their young siblings with the words and voice of a stern parent or mimicking women's gossip at the market. Children seemed well aware of adults' ambiguous authority, visible in their mocking imitations of parents and preachers, whose moral rebukes and admonitions they would exaggerate in humorous ways. Such performances revealed a strong communicative competence and creativity among the children, challenging and reinventing powerful registers to assert themselves among their peers. Language socialisation scholars have shown how interpretive reproduction and creative appropriation of local sociocultural schemes occur among children in all kinds of societies, forming a core part of their basic social, psychological and linguistic development (Cekaite et al. 2014; Evaldsson 2009). But in a rural, interdependent majority society like Hang'ombe, where families maintain a steep generational hierarchy and children's individual views and experiences receive limited adult attention, children's peer cultures and relationships might be especially significant to their appropriation of local practices, establishing their own voices and identities through hours and hours of chatting, fighting and joking. This capacity was perhaps most prominent in the tangible and symbolic realm of schooling, which I pursue in the next chapter.

Notes

1. Luyaba had carried the recorder around with her for a while, and no adults were present during this recording. The use of English is marked with bold.
2. Kupwa was usually played by two players at a time, but other children will often watch, waiting for their turn to join. Ten or more small stones were put in a hole, each player holding one additional stone in their hand. At his or her turn, the player must throw the stone in the air and catch it again while removing the stones from the hole, one with each throw. If the flying stone fell to the ground, the player lost this turn. The player who first managed to empty the hole would win.
3. I observed the children from about ten metres away while the recorder sat on the ground right next to them.
4. An earlier version of the subsequent analyses was published in the article Clemensen (2016).
5. Lushomo was carrying the recorder in her pocket while Khama and I observed from a distance.

❧ 4

THE DISTANT POWER OF SCHOOL
Academic Practices in Daily Life

A wati to nesi. A wati to dota. A wati to iJuniwa. A wati to Akata. [I want to be a nurse. I want to be a doctor. I want to be an engineer. I want to be an accountant.]
—Written in my notebook by Mududu, a 9-year-old girl

We really want to send our children to school. Why should they stay at home? We want them to know how to speak English, how to read, how to get money and count money. And then after that, to help their parents, buying blankets and covers, giving them money. But some of our children don't use their heads, and so they stop going to school.
—Love, 45-year-old mother of eight children and five grandchildren

By the age of seven, the large majority of Hang'ombe children entered the local basic school in Mbabala, joining age mates from the township and neighbouring villages. From early morning, hundreds of children walked along the dirt parts into the township, some covering distances of up to 8 km. Except during weekends and the month-long term breaks in December, May and August, children divided their days between homesteads and classrooms, each ascribing them with different roles and responsibilities. At home, matters of school were set aside in favour of household concerns, and in spite of teachers' requests, children rarely spent much time reading or doing homework exercises once leaving the school grounds. This did not imply that school was insignificant in children's out-of-school lives, however; I frequently observed children making direct or implicit academic references among peers, imitating teachers, writing letter-like symbols in the sand or singing songs about the alphabet and 'crossing the road'. Most children carried their uniforms with pride both in and out of school, and I often observed young children wailing at the morning departure of older siblings, wanting to go with them. With its connotations to modern lifestyles (*buumi bwasunu*), the school seemed both alluring and somewhat alien to most families.

Placed on the Eastern outskirts of Mbabala Township and shielded from the stir of the main street, Mbabala Basic School appeared calm even with hundreds of children running around or sitting in smaller groups during recess. Two whitewashed rectangular buildings of five classrooms each and a recently constructed smaller building for the grade eight and nine students surrounded a large courtyard centred by a large tree. About 750 students frequented the school in 2009, divided into nine grades with two classes on each level. With the last reform, 'Educating our future' (Zambian Ministry of Education 1996), school was officially free of charge from grades 1–7, which had increased national enrolment numbers quite drastically in the last fifteen years (Unesco 2012) and made Mbabala's gender balance close to even. To teachers' regret, increased enrolment had not brought equivalent financial support, and the supply of books, tables, chairs and other appliances was insufficient and rather worn. Due to shortage of both classrooms and teachers, classes were divided into morning and afternoon shifts, with higher grades dominating the afternoons. The 60m^2 classrooms contained parallel rows of wooden desks for forty students, a number often exceeded, particularly in early grades, leaving some students to sit on floor mats by the board.

In some ways, the school offered children social leeway, relieving them of household chores and allowing them to interact more freely with peers from other families and, in later years, to enter candid romantic relationships. On the other hand, the school sustained more meticulous codes of discipline than most children's homes: prior to each lesson, they had to await the teacher in gender-divided lines outside the classroom and greet her with 'Good morning, teacher! How are you?' before being allowed to enter. In class, they had to keep their gaze fixed towards the teacher and raise their hands and sometimes stand up before speaking on their own, which they had to do in a loud voice and with a distinct academic register. Once every term they went through extensive tests, the result of which were sometimes published on large sheets outside the teachers' room. Unlike the relative autonomy of children's out-of-school lives, school obliged them to remain seated in class throughout lessons, prohibiting them from entering other spaces. These rules and practices all underlined the school's status as a separate social domain.

As in most other schools in the region, lessons at Mbabala Basic followed a fixed set of teacher-managed routines. Topics of discussion varied across grade levels and learning areas, but most classes abided by a call-response or IRE structure – that is, a teacher-initiated question or call followed by an individual or collective student response explicitly or implicitly evaluated by the teacher by saying, for example, 'good' (mostly in English) or repeating the response loudly to the class, encouraging them to chorus along. To some observers, such routines might appear rigid and hierarchical, but as Cazden writes, the predictability might also enhance children's familiarity with the domain of school and thus their potential learning (Cazden 2001: 100). Even during the first days and weeks of the year, many new students appeared quite comfortable with their student role, answering teachers' questions in loud voices and laughing with their classmates during breaks. I frequently heard teachers address both younger and older students, telling them 'don't fear' (*mutanooyoowi*) or 'speak freely' (*kamwaanguluka kukanana*), requesting them to speak louder and more directly than they might normally do when addressing their parents or other adult members. Paradoxically, while maintaining a strictly regulated interaction practice, teachers tried to promote students' free expression in class, especially in higher grades, where they were encouraged to be critical of the presented texts and to create individual arguments of their own. The following extract depicts a grade two lesson of Oral English conducted in October 2008, when the class was following a programme referred to as 'happy class'.[1]

1. Teacher: **All right. What was our last lesson? What was our last lesson in 'happy class'?** Nciiyo cesu camamanino camu 'happy', cakali ciiyonzi? CakalicCiiyonzi? Twaluba?

    All right. What was our last lesson? What was our last lesson in 'happy class'? What was our last lesson in 'happy', what lesson was it? Have we forgotten? Have we?

2. Student: Kwiiya kupunda ciindi.

    We learnt how to tell time.

3. Teacher: Twakali kwiiya kupunda ciindi? **Sure?**

    We learnt how to tell time? Sure?

4. Student: [inaudible]

5. Teacher: **Okay. We have forgotten, okay? We looked at living things and? Non-living things.** Ede?

> *Okay. We have forgotten, okay? We looked at living things and? Non-living things. All right?*

6. Students: Mmm.

> *Yes.*

7. Teacher: **Can you mention any living things that you know?** Twakaiya zyintu zipona azitaponi, ede?

> *Can you mention any living things that you know? We learnt about living and non-living things, right?*

8. Students: Mmm.

> *Yes.*

9. Teacher: Ciiyo cesu camamanino, tee?

> *In our last lesson, right?*

10. Students: Mmm.

> *Yes.*

11. Teacher: Mpoonya ndaamba kuti amundaambile zyintu zyipona nzyomuzyi nywe. [To student] Pez?

> *Now I have told you to tell me living things that you know. [To student] Pez?*

12. Student: **'Cow'.**

> *'Cow'.*

13. Teacher: **'A cow', very good.** Aha?

> *'A cow', very good. Okay?*

14. Student: Bantu.

> *People.*

15. Teacher: Bantu, **yes, 'people'.** Aha?

> *People, yes, 'people'. Okay?*

16. Student: **'Goat'.**

> *'Goat'.*

17. Teacher: **'Goat', very good. Yes,** Vera? Twaluba ... Okay?

> *'Goat', very good. Yes, Vera? We have forgotten ... Okay?*

18. Student: **'Cat'.**

> *'Cat'.*

19. Teacher: **'A cat'. Aha?**
    'A cat'. Okay?

20. Student: **'Animals'.**
    'Animals'.

21. Teacher: **'Animals'. All right. There are a lot of living things. How about a tree? Is it not a living thing?** Ino cisamu cilapona naataciponi?
    'Animals'. All right. There are a lot of living things. How about a tree? Is it not a living thing? Is a tree a living thing or not?

22. Students: Cilapona.
    It is a living thing.

23. Teacher: Cilapona, **very good. Now, mention non-living things.** Amwaambe zyintu zyitaponi.
    It is a living thing, very good. Now, mention non-living things. Mention non-living things.

24. Student: Basisi!
    Teacher!

25. Teacher: **Yes.**
    Yes.

26. Student: Kasamu.
    A small tree.

27. Teacher: Kasamu kali buti? Twaamba kuti cisamu cilapona, ino waamba kuti 'kasamu'.
    What kind of small tree? We said that a tree is a living thing, now you have said 'a small tree'.

28. Student: Basisi!
    Teacher!

29. Teacher: Citaponi. **Yes?**
    Non-living things. Yes?

30. Student: Ibbwe.
    A stone.

31. Teacher: Ibbwe, **yes, a stone is a non-living thing.**
    Stone, yes, a stone is a non-living thing.

32. Student: Basisi!

> *Teacher!*

33. Teacher: Aha?
    Yes?

34. Student: Cisamu ciyumu.
    A dried tree.

35. Teacher: Cisamu ciyumu, **yes. A tree that has been cut is a non-living thing. Yes,** aha?
    A dried tree, yes. A tree that has been cut is a non-living thing. Yes, okay?

36. Student: **'Book'.**
    'Book'.

37. Teacher: **'A book', very good,** twalumba.
    'A book', very good', thank you.

38. Student: Basisi?
    Teacher?

39. Teacher: Aha?
    Yes?

40. Student: **'Pen'.**
    'Pen'.

41. Teacher: **'A pen', very good. All right,** twalumba ... **We are not looking at the same things; we are looking at different things. We are going to look at these things.**
    'A pen', very good. All right, thank you ...We are not looking at the same things; we are looking at different things. We are going to look at these things.

Like most class interactions at Mbabala, especially in lower grades, this interaction follows a fixed rhythmic pattern, sustained by the teacher's continuous calls for preset answers, which students try to give, and her subsequent evaluation or acknowledgement of these. The teacher, Mrs Bangweta, asks students to summarise their previous Oral English class with her, centring on the scientific categories of 'living things' (*zyintu zipona*, lines 5–22) and 'non-living things' (*zyintu zitaponi*, lines 23–41), which they are encouraged to exemplify through familiar references, like 'goat', 'cow', 'stone', 'tree' or 'book'. Shifting continuously between English and chiTonga and translating both her own and students' utterances, she seeks to familiarise them with a language they are likely to have been acquainted with in the media or among foreigners in the township but may rarely be spoken in their homes. The students first respond somewhat reluctantly, perhaps struggling to figure out the correct answers and name these – in English – on their own, but they generally appear eager to participate, prompted by Bangweta's encouraging tag questions mainly in chiTonga, like *ede?* ('all right?'), *tee?* ('right?'), *aha?* ('okay?') and the recurrent acknowledgement in English, 'very good'. In their out-of-school lives, Hang'ombe children were hardly ever asked to name or categorise specific things or phenomena, neither in chiTonga nor English, and especially not those physically absent in the room. As we saw in Chapter 2, children acquired basic competences and chores mainly through the quiet observation and imitation of adults, and parents or other adults rarely asked children questions, unless they were rebuking them or needed tangible information from the child about something he or she had done, seen or heard. Prefixed or known answer-inquiries like above – what sociolinguist Basil Bernstein famously called the school's *decontextualised code* (Bernstein 1973) – was an educational practice more or less exclusively presented to children in classrooms. Older children who had gained confidence in the school's customs could sometimes be observed playing school and mimicking or mocking teachers' monotonous, solemn voices and registers, perhaps addressing younger siblings as insecure 'students' in the style depicted above. But such playful mimicry only seemed to emphasise the school's detached ambience in local society.

Language socialisation scholars have described how children's early school socialisation largely revolves around their introduction to and gradual acquisition of a specific linguistic register that may differ significantly from the language and interactive practices prevailing in their homes (Baquedano-López and Kattan 2008; Figueroa and Baquedano-López 2017). Such difference has been observed especially among children coming from ethnically and socio-economically marginalised groups in both Western and non-Western settings, as schools all over the world tend to adopt and promote the social and linguistic norms practised mainly by upper- and middle-class families (Avineri et al. 2015; Heath 1983). Since the 1960s, manifold educational programmes have been launched to make academic knowledge more accessible to minoritised children by bridging the so-called 'language gap'; for example, by training parents to modify their language and speech patterns or read books to children (Avineri and Johnson 2015), or by allowing children to speak their native language in class, mostly for an introductory phase of 1–3 years, in settings where the predominant language differs from the language(s) spoken by a large number of students. The latter approach has been assumed in many postcolonial countries since the 1960s, varying in scale and ambition but aimed basically at easing minority children's adaption to standardised language and literacy practices (Alidou et al. 2006; Haddad 2008). In Zambia, the *Primary Reading Programme* was implemented nationwide in the early 2000s with the explicit aim of 'bridging the language gap' especially in rural areas, allowing children to speak one of seven regional languages in class for their first three years of schooling, after which they were expected to perform mainly in English (Sampa 2005). This programme was still employed in lower grades at Mbabala Basic and other schools in the province during my stay in 2008–9, manifesting in frequent code-mixes by both teachers and students like in the 'happy class' lesson of Oral English above. As I have discussed elsewhere (Clemensen 2010), the introduction of systematic, mother tongue-based teaching and learning methods was likely to enhance children's class participation and reduce early experiences of alienation. Like linguistic ethnographers studying school interactions in other parts of Africa (Brock-Utne, Desai and Qorro 2006; Heugh 2009), I observed how teachers' familiar language use elicited more confident and elaborate answers from students than the use of English, like above, and how the use of chiTonga allowed teachers to establish intimate relationships with students, calling them *basa* ('dear ones'), joking with them and making little comments on their responses. Mbabala teachers were highly aware of these advantages, and the ones I observed all practised a mixture of English and chiTonga, even in higher grades, in order to help students understand and participate in class. However, the overriding dominance of English in national exams and the remaining school system made it hard for teachers to maintain the use of chiTonga as more than a symbolic gesture.

A Risky Investment

Among Hang'ombe families, few adults had completed more than seven years of schooling, and daily life seemed to require little direct use of academic knowledge, apart from occasional Bible readings and the keeping of household accounts. Unless called upon by the headmaster, parents rarely visited the school grounds, and teachers told me how only a handful had helped moulding bricks for the planned building of classrooms for grade eight and nine students in

2008, in spite of urgent requests. Such seeming lack of involvement might be ascribed to parents' busy workdays, along with a generally low familiarity with the language and methodologies presented to children at school, especially in higher grades. However, it might also reflect a more deep-rooted disappointment with the basic school system. Having seen young locals return unemployed and empty-handed after finishing secondary school or even college, many parents seemed unsure of the school's potentials for actual change in their lives. Relying heavily on children's workforce, they found it increasingly futile to send them off to school, asking themselves if children – and they themselves – might not be better off preparing themselves for a life as farmers and housewives.

When interviewed by 'educated people' like Khama and myself, however, most parents expressed hopes of their children completing school (*kumanizya cikolo*) – grade twelve – and eventually gaining paid employment to sustain themselves and their families. Expressions like 'the goodness of school' (*bubotu bwa cikolo*) appeared in casual conversations, often linked with hopes of children eventually 'mixing with White people' in Lusaka or London, exempt from the hardships of village life. Such hopes were warranted by the political discourse prevailing among both national and international stakeholders – for example, the United Nation's 2015 Millennium Goals (Unesco 2000) – claiming that school intrinsically lead to social mobility and increased quality of life. This discourse was also endorsed by local authorities both in and outside of school. 74-year-old senior headman Noah spoke to me about school perceptions among local families:

> A lot of parents have knowledge about school now, and normally we don't have to whip them to send their children to school. Out of a hundred people, maybe one person doesn't send his children. Then we [senior headmen] have to deal with that person, so we send out a messenger and tell him to come and see us. We tell him what we heard from the school: 'I was told by the teacher that your children are not going to school. That is wrong.' We tell him, 'School is good, because your child is able to mix with others, different people. They will be able to talk to White people. You can't go outside, to Europe or whatever, unless you are in school.'

Among the families I observed, parents tended to encourage children's schooling most fully for the first seven years, finding tangible use in their basic acquisition of literacy, math, English and home economics. Passing the prestigious grade seven exam enhanced both boys' and girls' marital potential along with their entire family's local status. As children reached puberty, however, other interests became increasingly evident both to them and their families. According to my

census in late 2009, about 60 per cent of Hang'ombe girls left school
before reaching grade nine, mostly due to pregnancy and/or increased
obligations in the household. Between 2008–9, only 12 per cent of
18-year-old girls – including daughters no longer living in the village –
had completed grade twelve. Boys tended to reach slightly higher
levels of schooling, with 55 per cent of 22-year-old Hang'ombe boys
having passed their grade nine exam by January 2009 and about 20 per
cent of them having completed grade twelve. While the social pressure
of early marriage and parenthood might be lighter, expectations of
financial independency seemed to create an equal counterweight
against the continued schooling of Hang'ombe boys. As an illustration
of how many families approached the realm of schooling, the extract
below was recorded one January evening in 2009 in the kitchen of Lila
and Levias Hambuulo, who generally presented themselves as highly
engaged in their children's schooling, striving to support the secondary
schooling of their oldest daughter Chipo (17). At one point in the
conversation, Lila asked her 9-year-old daughter Luyando about her
first day of grade three at Mbabala Basic. Luyando's father Levias and
her 10-year-old brother Oscar soon joined the conversation:[2]

1. Lila [to Luyando]: Kondaambila zyacitika sunu kucikolo?
   Tell me, what happened in school today?

2. Luyando: Bayi nibanjila mu class yesu, bandibuzya zyina.
   When the teacher came in class, she asked me my name.

3. Lila: Ati nzi?
   What did she say?

4. Luyando: Balaamba ategwa, **'What is your name?'**
   She asked me, 'What is your name?'

5. Lila: Mpoonya yebo ategwa nzi?
   What did you reply?

6. Luyando: Mpoonya ategwa nzi? Me ndati, **'My name is Luyando Hambuulo'.**
   What did I reply? I said, 'My name is Luyando Hambuulo'.

7. Lila: Mpoonya ati nzi?
   What did she say then?

8. Luyando: Mpoonya ategwa 'Good' ati 'Kokkala'.
   Then she replied 'Good' and said 'Sit down'.

9. Lila: Ino mbaani bamuiisya?

Who is your teacher?

10. Luyando: Mbaa Chilungu ... Muli bazyi ba Chilungu?

   It is Mrs Chilungu ... Do you know Mrs Chilungu?

11. Lila: Mbibaali kumuiisya a mu giledi one?

   Is she the one who taught you in grade one?

12. Luyando: Peepe. Kai mu giledi one bakazyootuisya ba Malala.
   Mpoonya baleka mpoonya ciindi comwe kwatuyiisya ba Lwiindi.
   Mpoonya bazyooleka mpoonya ...

   No. In grade one, Mrs Malala taught us, then she stopped.
   Thereafter, Mr Lwiindi taught us one time. Then he stopped ...

13. Lila: Kwamuiisya bani?

   Who taught you [that one time]?

14. Luyando: Ba Lwiindi ba headmaster. Mpoonya bazyooleka, mpoonya
   kwatuiisya ba mrs Manyando.

   Mr Lwiindi, the headmaster. Then he stopped, then Mrs
   Manyando taught us.

15. Oscar: Mbaa Halwiindi – buya mbezyi. Ati tabali 'ba Lwiindi' ati 'mbaa
   Halwiindi'.

   It is Mr Halwiindi – that is what I know. She [Luyando] shouldn't
   have said 'Mr Lwiindi' but 'Mr Halwiindi'.

16. Levias: Ba headmaster?

   The headmaster?

17. Oscar: liyi.

   Yes.

18. Luyando: 'Mbaa Lwiindi'.

   It is 'Mr Lwiindi'.

19. Oscar: Mebo ndizyi kuti 'mbaa Halwiindi'. Waloati mbaa 'Lwiindi'.

   I know that he is 'Mr Halwiindi'. But she [Luyando] says it is
   'Lwiindi'.

[The family members all remain quiet for a while after this and then go
on to discuss other issues.]

Lila asks Luyando what happened that day at school (line 1); about
the teacher's specific instructions (lines 3, 7) and Luyando's response
to these (line 5). As such, Lila appears interested in the tangible course

of her daughter's schooling, but after a few brief replies (lines 2, 4, 6, 8) she leaves the subject, moving on to Luyando's new teacher (lines 9, 11), a topic that occupies the whole family for their remaining conversation (lines 9–19). Luyando lists three different teachers (lines 12, 14) but is corrected by her brother Oscar on one of these, Mr Halwiindi, who is also the current headmaster of Mbabala Basic (line 15). The headmaster's name calls the attention of the children's father, Levias, who wants to make sure Halwiindi actually taught Luyando (line 16) – whereby Oscar and Luyando begin the discussion of the headmaster's name again (lines 18–19). Like most of the families I observed, Lila and her family members seem particularly concerned with the *formal* aspects of schooling – teachers' names and statuses, the passing of grades, sanctioning of rules and reproduction of school-associated phrases like 'What is your name?', 'Good' and *'Kokkala'* ('Sit down') (lines 4, 8). In line with villagers' apparent concern with social norms of speech, dress and reciprocity, schooling was discussed mainly in terms of social representation. Local teachers' alleged misdemeanours were popular topics of discussion, like Mr Tolokesi, who had recently taken a second wife in a nearby village while continuing marital relations with his first wife in the township. Watching him ride his bike on a weekly basis between these two homes, members disdainfully commented how a respected authority like Tolokesi ought to remain a moral role model (*mukonzyanyo*) and abstain from a backwards tradition like polygyny.

Underlining this symbolic power of schooling, the display of academic proficiencies, like the use of English or technical discourse, formed a vital parameter of status and respect among many villagers, overriding more traditional deeds of farming and housekeeping. This was also apparent in an interaction I observed between 38-year-old Minivah Hang'ombe and her two visiting aunts, 46-year-old Dorothy and her 37-year-old co-wife Edinah, both married to Minivah's maternal uncle, Leonard. Along with Minivah's oldest daughters, 11-year-old Talala and 9-year-old Mududu, Khama and I were sitting as quiet listeners to the interaction, whose focus on education was triggered by our research project:[3]

1. Dorothy [to Khama]: nga ulazyilemba ezyi?
   Do you write these recordings in books?

2. Khama: liyi.
   Yes.

3. Dorothy: Ulalemba?

   You write [analyse]?

4. Khama: iyi, ciyootutolela mazuba manji kuzyilemba.

   Yes, it will take us a long time to write [to analyse the recordings].

5. Minivah: Iiyi, mulimo mupati.

   Yes, it is a very big job.

6. Dorothy: Lwiiyo ncintu cikatazya. Ciyanda kucita zyintu zyinji kutegwa muntu aiye.

   Education is a difficult thing. It takes a lot of things [effort] for one to become educated.

7. Minivah: Iiyi, cilakatazya.

   Yes, it is very difficult.

8. Dorothy [sighing]: Lwiiyo …

   Education …

9. Edinah: Lwiiyo lulakatazya.

   Education is very difficult.

10. Minivah: Swebo notukkede kumunzi [notutaiyi] tukkede kabotu.

    We who stay at home [without going to school] are well off [comfortable].

11. Dorothy: Kabotu.

    We're well off.

12. Edinah: Twamana ndiswe notupengede.

    But we have a lot of problems.

13. Dorothy: iyi, ndiswe notupengede.

    Yes, we have a lot of problems.

14. Edinah: iyi.

    Yes.

15. Dorothy: Pele kulima.

    We just farm.

16. Minivah: iyi, masimpe. Pele kuyeeya kulima.

    Yes, it is true. We only think about farming.

17. Dorothy: Akuyeeya kuti ino sunu ndajika nzi.

    The other thing we think of is what to cook.

18. Edinah: Nzyezyintu nzyotuyeeya.

    Those are the only things we think of.

19. Edinah: Cimwi ciindi twakainkide kumuunda kuyoobika fertiliser. Nitwakamana kubikka fertiliser, tiiyakawa.

    A long time ago we went to the maize field to apply fertiliser. After applying fertiliser, it didn't rain.

20. Minivah: Unhu?

    Yes?

21. Edinah: Kwa nsondo zyobilo tiiyakawa. Aboobo, fertiliser tiiwakanyebuluka. Mulumi wesu wakatwaambila kuti tuubwezelele fertiliser mumapopwe.

    For three weeks it didn't rain. As a result, the fertiliser didn't dissolve into the soil. Our husband told us to go and pick up the fertiliser from the maize.

22. Dorothy [jokingly]: Mulumi wesu wamaleele wakatwaambila kuti amukaubwezelele fertiliser.

    Our miraculous husband told us to recollect the fertiliser.

23. Minivah [surprised]: Peepe!

    No!

24. Dorothy: Masimpe. Eci cakacitika nitwakali kukkala ku Batoka. Mane twakaubwezelela fertiliser mumuunda.

    It is true. This happened when we were living in Batoka. We had to recollect the fertiliser from the maize crops.

25. Edinah: Mane twakaubwezelela fertiliser mumapopwe. Ino ndakanyema. Ndakayeeya kuti neeliy iide.

    We had to recollect the fertiliser from the maize crops. I was very annoyed. I regretted not having gone to school.

26. Dorothy: Kuti nindakaliyiide, nindatakabwezelela fertiliser.

    If we were educated, we wouldn't have recollected the fertiliser.

27. Edinah: Kuzwa leelyo, bantu bakauuzyika kuti 'muunda wabatayiide'.

    Since then, people gave the name 'the field of uneducated people' to our field.

28. Minivah: iyi, kutayiya mapenzi. Kuti koyiide, inga kokkala buyo mu office.

> *Yes, lack of education is a problem. If you are educated, you*
> *just sit in an office.*

29. Dorothy: Kutayiya ceetela mapenzi. Iiyi, kuti koyiide, inga kokkala buyo
mu office.

> *Lack of education brings problems. Yes, if you are educated,*
> *you just sit in an office.*

[After this, the women remain quiet for a while.]

Initially, Dorothy asks Khama about our writing (*lemba*) of recordings –
that is, the transcription and analysis of data she expects us to conduct
(lines 1, 3). Khama tells her the recordings 'will take a long time to
write' (line 4), causing Minivah to note how the study 'is a very big
job' (line 5). This evokes a longer exchange among the three women on
the hardships of schooling (lines 6–9) and how people who never went
to school like them are 'well off' (*kabotu*) – that is, comfortable in not
having to study (lines 10–11) – but also how their lack of schooling brings
them 'a lot of problems' (*notupengede*, lines 12–14), including physically
exhausting work in the fields and a constant preoccupation with feeding
their families (lines 15–18). Edinah and Dorothy then recount how their
'miraculous husband' Leonard once made them recollect small bits
of fertiliser that were lying undissolved on one of the family's maize
fields after three weeks of drought, thus humiliating the two women
as both poor and subordinate to their husband and making both of
them regret not having gone to school (lines 19–27). Local families soon
began mocking Leonard and his family by referring to their maize
field as *muunda wabatayiide* ('the field of uneducated people', line 27),
underlining the school's symbolic power in village life.

As we have seen before, people generally maintained high social
and moral ideals in everyday discourse, lauding the blessings
of church and the goodness of schooling. Appointing stigmas of
stupidity or lack of education to unfortunate people like Leonard and
his wives above could serve to enhance the self-esteem of neighbours
and extended family members, even if they might have had little
schooling themselves. In line with the earlier example of Khama and
his family members' sharing their negative impression of foreign
workers, the three women above continuously repeat and extend each
other's utterances (lines 6–7, 8–9, 12–13, 17–18, 21–22, 24–25), thus
aligning themselves and supporting each other around the mutual
experience of formal education being both 'a big job' (lines 5–10)
and a privilege, posing a challenge for poor subsistence farmers like
themselves (lines 25–29).

A more subtle illustration of school's local power was the way in which people with some level of schooling frequently inserted English words into their chiTonga-dominated speech with friends or family members, candidly displaying their academic proficiencies. Such self-promotion might backfire, however, as apparent in the following brief interaction, recorded around a family fire in the Mweemba homestead in late 2008, when 32-year-old Roy, his 26-year-old nephew Alfred and 65-year-old father Milo were discussing the moral implications of insulting speech. At one point, Roy used the English term 'infect' while arguing how a righteous person should be able to address sensitive issues, like bodily and sexual questions, in conversations with others without being judged as immoral. Rather than answering, Alfred stopped to question his uncle's terminology:[4]

1. Roy: Kuti muntu uutatukani waamba cintu cibaanka cilatukana, inga tacibaciti **infect**, bantu batali kabotu balacipandulula bumbi, mbuli kuti nkutukana.

   > *If someone who does not [normally] insult says something which appears as an insult, it [what they have said] will not infect them, but bad people interpret things which are meant to teach, as insults.*

2. Alfred: no bbala **'infect'** lyaamba nzi?
   > *What does the word 'infect' mean?*

3. Roy: Hee?
   > *What?*

4. Alfred: **'Infect'?**
   > *'Infect'?*

5. Roy: **'Infect'.** Caamba kuti nokuba kuti waambilwa cintu, kwiina mbonvwa.

   > *'Infect'. It means that even if you are told something, you don't feel anything.*

6. Alfred and Milo: Ino **'affect'?**
   > *How about 'affect'?*

7. Roy: Caamba cintu comwe.
   > *It means the same.*

8. Alfred: Peepe, zyiliindene.
   > *No, they are different.*

9. Roy [to Alfred]: Amutwaambile lwiindano. Mwaanzya mukuwa masyikati ati, **'Good evening'**. Teem-wabona? Mponya ati Mwalubizya ati nimwaamba kuti, **'Good afternoon'**.

> *Tell us the difference. You greeted the White lady in the afternoon by saying 'Good evening'. Have you seen? Then she told you that since it was still afternoon you should say 'Good afternoon'.*

[Everyone remains quiet for a while after this, after which the conversation moves on to other topics.]

This extract reveals the frequent teasing and playful mocking played out around family fires. Assisted by his grandfather Milo, Alfred challenges Roy's English terminology, suggesting he use *'affect'* rather than *'infect'* in his statement (lines 2, 4, 6). Roy claims the two terms to be synonymous (line 7) and reminds Alfred how he himself had his English corrected by 'the White lady' earlier that day[5] (line 9) – that is, me jokingly telling Alfred to say *'Good afternoon'* rather than *'Good evening'* during our visit earlier that same day in reply to his correction of my faulty chiTonga – which seems to end the discussion above. Although no direct references to schooling or education were made, interactions like the one above may be seen as a negotiation of power and status between family members, based on their respective academic proficiency. English thus often served as a powerful performative tool, even in situations having little to do with school.

School's Distinctive Powers

Many Hang'ombe children seemed to apply an equally strong symbolic power to schooling, saturated with dreams of wealth and recognition. This became apparent in a small writing assignment I gave to a class of twenty grade eight Mbabala students in late 2008 in collaboration with their English teacher. I included the question *'What would you like to do when you grow up?'*. Here are a few representative answers:

Irene (female, 13): **'I want to finish school and help my family when I get work.'**

Fiona (female, 13): **'If I pass my grade 12 exam I want to be an accountant.'**

Editor (male, 14): **'I want to be a teacher so that I [can] help my mother and my father.'**

Lovely (female, 13): **'I want to be a teacher. I [would] like a family after [I] finish school and find a job.'**

Boyd (male, 14): **'I would like to be a doctor or whatever job it will be found at that time, so that I will help my family, other people or my relatives'.**

Eunice (female, 13): **'I want three or four houses at South Africa'.**

Choolwe (male, 14): **'When I grow up I would like to be a teacher'.**

As appears, many students perceived schooling as a collective enterprise, imbuing them with both the possibility and responsibility of reciprocating their families' efforts through material support. Interestingly, girls and boys expressed similar vocational dreams, most likely inspired by the pictures and stories presented to them in class. However, such dreams were rarely pursued through focused school work neither by boys or girls, as their out-of-school time was dominated by household chores and concerns. This was reflected in their school performances, as Hang'ombe children often appeared quiet, distracted and subdued in class. One teacher compared the teaching of village children to 'carrying something heavy' due to their alleged inproficiency in English, the main medium of school instruction. Outside of school, however, I often heard Hang'ombe children experiment with their school proficiencies among peers, telling stories, citing proverbs, singing songs and employing complex academic discourse both in English and chiTonga:[6]

One afternoon in early March 2009, 9-year-old Disteria and her 7-year-old brother Munsanje were walking to their cousins' homestead about a kilometre away to pick up rapeseeds from their aunt for their mother. Passing a tree full of bush fruits, Munsanje asked his sister about them, wanting to know if they were edible. Disteria identified the fruits as food (*ncilyo*) and started counting them, displaying both the abundance of fruits and her own counting skills, which were soon imitated by young Munsanje. Disteria then mentioned their cousin, 11-year-old Lidea, who lived in a nearby village and had visited the children's homestead with her family the day before. According to Disteria, Lidea claimed to be attending grade five, even though her cousins both knew her as a fourth grader at the local school:

1. Munsanje [looking at a fruit]: Ino eci ncilyo nzi, nobantu?
   What food is this, you people?

2. Disteria [counting fruits]:   Awa ncilyo, alya ncilyo, **one, two, three, four, five ...**

> *Here is food, here is food, one, two, three, four, five ...*

3. Munsanje [imitating Disteria]:   **One, two, three, four, five ...**

> *One, two, three, four, five ...*

4. Disteria [annoyed]: Jilo, Lidea wakaamba kuti ngu grade five.

> *Yesterday, Lidea said she was in grade five.*

5. Munsanje: Iiyi, mwaiya.

> *Yes, [that is the grade] she is learning [attending].*

6. Disteria: Ulabeja.

> *It is a lie.*

7. Munsanje: Ategwa ni?

> *She said what?*

8. Disteria: Ategwa grade five.

> *She said grade five.*

9. Munsanje: Ategwa nzi?

> *What did she say?*

10. Disteria: Ategwa wiiya grade five.

> *She said she is in grade five.*

11. Munsanje: Nceamba kuti ulabeja.

> *I'm saying, it is a lie.*

12. Disteria [annoyed]: Ede mbombubo mbaakaamba kuti.

> *But that is what she was saying.*

13. Munsanje: Ambebo mbindakanvwa jilo kumazuba, iiyi.

> *That is also what I heard yesterday evening, yes.*

14. Disteria: Uyeeya kuti ulicenjede kwiinda ndiswe. Ulayanda kulibonesya.

> *She thinks she is smarter than us. She wants to show off.*

15. Munsanje: Iiyi, uyanda kulibonesya.

> *Yes, she wants to show off.*

Whether true or not, Disteria's accusation of Lidea having lied about attending a higher grade reveals the social significance that

Disteria herself ascribes to school's institutional hierarchy. Along with age, schooling served as the overriding parameter of social and moral distinction among all the children I observed, irrespective of their school grades and varying socio-economic backgrounds. Equal to most adults, children associated schooling with moral superiority, ascribing increasing moral standards to children as they attended higher grades. Disteria thus presents Lidea's claim as highly immoral; not only was she – an older child – lying, but she was using the lie to assert herself as intellectually and morally superior to her cousins, both of whom attended lower grades. This is also visible in Disteria's final analysis, claiming that Lidea wanted to 'show off' (*kulibonesya*, line 14). Munsanje, however, seems more concerned with pleasing his older sister, Disteria, than with the issue of Lidea. He first confirms that Lidea indeed attends grade five (line 5 above), but when Disteria states her dismay against Lidea's claim (line 6), Munsanje soon aligns himself with her, agreeing that 'it is a lie' (line 11) and that Lidea indeed wants to 'show off' (line 15). Munsanje's ongoing attempts to align himself with his older sister (lines 3, 11, 13, 14) seem to reveal both respect and fear towards her, considering her age and educational status; Disteria is in third grade while Munsanje has only recently entered grade one. At his relatively young age, 7-year-old Munsanje may be unsure of how to evaluate the claims of an older child like Lidea, and so he chooses to align himself with his older sister, not risking the potential defeat and humiliation of challenging her. Imitating Disteria's counting at the beginning of the extract (lines 2–3), Munsanje manages to pay her respect while at the same time showing his own counting skills. Interestingly, Disteria blames her cousin Lidea for 'showing off', a practice that could equally be applied to her. However, by claiming to attend a higher grade, especially in front of peers well aware of the falseness of this claim, Lidea seems to have exceeded prevailing norms of modesty and reliability. Disteria thus familiarises her younger brother with the social power of academic discourse, along with the necessity of handling such power with great care.

As another type of children's school reference, I often heard them practising their ability to tell the time. Few children had direct access to clocks, except perhaps when glancing at the cell phones of their parents; but like adults, a child might use the position of the sun and the regular unfolding of daily routines to estimate the time of day. During school days, children – and parents – had to know the approximate time in order to reach school in the township before 8 AM. But though adults rarely displayed punctuality, I frequently heard children announcing the exact time, like '14 hours' or '10 hours', and associating these times with their daily routines. These announcements might not be accurate, neither in terms of the time of speaking or conducting the actual chore – but like the use of English, they might serve to indicate the speaker's level of education, revealing his or her ability to decode and categorize the world accordingly. In the brief interaction below, 9-year-old Brenda asks her 7-year-old sister Miyoba to escort her to the well to draw water. Miyoba agrees to come but then asks her older sister *when* she might go to the well; a question indicating, but not insisting on, a request for an exact time:

1. Brenda [to Miyoba]: Ino ambebo uyoondigwasya [ndaakwiinka kuteka meenda]?
    Will you help me also [when I go to draw water]?

2. Miyoba: Iiyi. Ino wiinka lili?
    Yes. When are you going?

3. Brenda [insecurely]: Ccita … Lino ngu **14 hours.**
    I don't know … It is now 14 hours.

4. Miyoba [confidently]: Mbuleeno? Iiyi, ngu **14 hours.**
    Now? Yes, it is 14 hours.

5. Brenda [insecurely]: Cakali ciindi nzi jilo nimwakali kuyooteka meenda?
    What time was it when you went to draw water yesterday?

6. Miyoba: Cakali **14 hours.**
    It was 14 hours.

7. Brenda: Ulabeja, kwakali ba five bobile. Cakali **75 hours.**
    You're lying. The five were two [there were two fives]. It was 75 hours.

8. Miyoba: Tocizyi. Taakwe **75 hours.**
    You don't know that. There is no such thing as 75 hours.

9. Brenda: Ndileke endikke ndilamulomba Malilwe andigwasye kuteka meenda kuleka zyeezyo.
    Leave me alone. I'll ask Malilwe to help me pour water instead.

[Miyoba does not respond, and the girls remain quiet for a while after this.]

Miyoba's opening question (line 2) could be seen as an innocent request to know whether Brenda is planning to leave for the well soon – but also be as a challenge on Miyoba's behalf, urging her older sister to state an exact time for her planned enterprise. Brenda responds that 'it is now 14 hours' (line 3), revealing her knowledge of time while perhaps indicating that the two of them should leave soon to avoid being late for the preparation of supper. Miyoba confirms this hour (line 4), showing that she, like her older sister, is well aware of the time. When Brenda asks what time Miyoba herself went to the well the previous day (line 5), Miyoba gives the same reply as Brenda did before: '14 hours' (line 6). Brenda, however, rejects this reply, telling her sister she is 'lying', that 'the five were two' and that it was in fact '75 hours' when Miyoba went to the well (line 7). This response indicates that Brenda – and Miyoba – has access to a digital clock, most likely a cell phone, on which 'two fives' may appear (e.g. 1:55 hours). Brenda' claim that 'it was 75 hours' reveals a certain insecurity in her mastery of the clock, but it also underlines what is actually at stake in this interaction between the two sisters; namely determining which of them is the more educated – and thus, more intelligent and powerful – in this case based on the possession and display of prestigious school-associated knowledge like the clock and the categorisation of events. This is also evident in Miyoba's response, 'You don't know that' (line 8), by which she dismisses Brenda's suspicion and cuts her older sister down to size, telling her that 'There is no such thing as 75 hours' (line 8). In her final remark, Brenda seems to recognise her defeat, telling her younger sister to 'leave [her] alone' – and that she will ask Malilwe, the girls' 11-year-old niece, to accompany her to the well instead.

Although no direct reference to schooling or education is made, this interaction can be seen as a power negotiation between two young girls, based on their respective display of academic knowledge and their attempts to position both themselves and each other in regard to this knowledge. It shows how children may apply new meanings to school-associated practices like the announcement of time, using them as powerful performative tools. If only for a short while, 7-year-old Miyoba has managed to defeat her older sister in the generational hierarchy. While the display of punctuality might not concur with practical circumstances, talking about time in terms of dates and hours might thus serve to present oneself as a modern, urban and educated person.

Perhaps more than any other practice, children associated schooling with the experience and gradual acquisition of *English* – a language that was otherwise rarely used outside the township and local church.

When playing by themselves, I often heard children use English or English-sounding words, even if few of them were able to have an actual conversation in English. This appears in the following interaction among five children seated around the kitchen fire, chatting and cooking dinner while their mother/aunt is out in the field. One of the girls, 8-year-old Lushomo, had just finished preparing a fish for the family supper, while her cousin, 13-year-old Mutinta, and her sister, 11-year-old Talala, had chopped greens. The girls' 20-year-old male cousin Sinyimbwe was also present along with Lushomo and Talala's 3-year-old brother Habeenzu:

1. Mutinta [to Lushomo, mockingly]: Ino Lushomo walijikide. [to Talala] Na, naitwa kuti ndish nzi eyi, Talala?

   Lushomo, you have cooked so nicely. What dish is this, Talala?

2. Talala [in low voice]: Ccita naitwa kuti ni dish nzi eyi.

   I don't know what this dish is.

3. Mutinta [laughing]: **Boiling system stroke frying.**

   Boiling system stroke frying.

4. Lushomo [to Mutinta]: Ino ndime ndali kujika na yawe?

   Is it my cooking [you're referring to]?

5. Sinyimbwe [to all]: Taifuya buya, kwiina naifulaya buya boiling ndebe.

   She [Lushomo] did not fry it, she was just boiling it.

6. Mutinta: Ndaamba buya mboibede. **Boiling system stroke frying.**

   I'm just saying it as it is. Boiling system stroke frying.

7. Talala: Inga mbuli kuti saladi yavwula.

   There was too much cooking oil.

8. Sinyimbwe: Yabila maningi.

   It boiled for a long time.

9. Talala: Inga mbuli kuti saladi yavwula.

   There was too much cooking oil.

10. Habeenzu: Mutinta, Mutinta!

    Mutinta, Mutinta!

11. Mutinta: Lushomo, kuti babuzyigwa kuti ni **method** nzi eyi, inga waamba kuti nzi?

> *Lushomo, if you are asked about the method you used to cook, what will you say?*

12. Lushomo: Nkuti 'kwiina'.
    I will say 'nothing'.

13. Sinyimbwe: Nkwaamba kuti 'ndijika cikuwa-kuwa'.
    You can simply say 'I cook like a town person'.

14. Lushomo: Nkuti ni **design.**
    I can say it is a design.

15. Talala [to Mutinta]: Ino kujika kuli **design?**
    Is there any design in cooking?

16. Mutinta [to Talala]: Kuti **design?**
    She said it is a design?

17. Talala: Iiyi.
    Yes.

18. Mutinta [to Talala, mockingly]: Zyacikuwa-cikuwa ezyi nzyizyakwe. Nzyakuli zyacikuwacikuwa ezyi? Hee?
    This town way of cooking of hers. Where is that town way of cooking from? Huh?

This interaction focuses on Lushomo's cooking, which Mutinta mocks, as Lushomo has accidentally fried the fish by adding too much cooking oil to the boiling water. Children often discussed the conduct of different social and work-related practices, observing each other's speech, actions and personal appearance and evaluating these against the social practices and precepts prevailing around them. Like previous examples, the extract above can be seen as an investigation and negotiation among the children, not only of a tangible household practice like cooking but also of how to talk about it, presenting oneself as an educated person. The interaction is led by 13-year-old Mutinta, who appears both linguistically and socially more confident than the others – most likely due to her age, her status as the most highly educated (grade eight) and the fact that she has grown up in the large town of Livingstone, which gives her more regular exposure to English and other town-like practices and lifestyles than her cousins.

Mutinta starts off by making a sarcastic comment to Lushomo – and her peers – of how Lushomo has cooked so nicely and asks Lushomo's 11-year-old sister Talala for the name of this unconventional dish (line

1). Talala seems unsure of how to respond and tells Mutinta that she does not 'know what this dish is' (line 2), implicitly acknowledging her cousin's ridicule of Lushomo. Mutinta then employs the English expression, *'boiling system stroke frying'* (line 3), which can be seen as reference to an academic discourse broadly associated with schooling. I frequently heard the English term *'system'* applied among teachers and other educated people in the area, like a veterinarian talking about 'the farming system' or a social worker telling me about the local 'family system'. Above, Mutinta adds even more complexity to her description of Lushomo's cooking by comparing 'the system of boiling' with 'the system of frying', using the English term 'stroke' to show the incompatibility between the two. 8-year-old Lushomo appears familiar with this expression, asking Mutinta (in chiTonga), if she is referring to Lushomo's cooking (line 4). 20-year-old Sinyimbwe then steps in and defends his young cousin, telling Mutinta – and the others – how Lushomo 'did not fry it, she was just boiling it' (line 5). As an early school leaver with a limited proficiency in English, Sinyimbwe might experience Mutinta's mocking of Lushomo's cooking as targeted more broadly towards uneducated people like himself.

11-year-old Talala makes a more matter-of-fact evaluation of Lushomo's cooking job, stating how there was too much cooking oil (line 7) – again implicitly aligning herself with her older cousin. Mutinta carries on mocking Lushomo, repeating her declaration of 'boiling system stroke frying' (line 6) and later posing the sarcastic question: 'Lushomo, if you are asked about the *method* you used to cook, what will you say?' (line 11), again evoking an academic discourse, this time by using a scientific English term. Sinyimbwe suggests that Lushomo answers 'I cook like a town person' (line 13), reflecting the social distinction between town persons (*cikuwakuwa*) and villagers (*basiminzi*), one commonly noted by children as well as adults. Even if this distinction might sometimes be used in critiques of the (im)moral practices of people in the township, being referred to as a *cikuwa-kuwa* (literally, a townsman or an urbaner) was usually regarded as a compliment, pointing to the person's wealth and modern manners in terms of clothes, shoes, speech and the possession of modern items like a cell phone or TV. In line with this, applying cooking oil to one's cooking was generally seen as a sign of wealth and sophistication, and although Lushomo might have added *too much* cooking oil to the fish pot, compared to prevailing standards, Sinyimbwe reminds his peers of how this might be perceived as better than adding little or no cooking oil at all. Interestingly, both Mutinta and Sinyimbwe thus evoke connotations of urbanity, modernity and formal education in their respective attempts to assert both the quality of Lushomo's cooking and, implicitly, their own status in the group. Lushomo joins them in this negotiation, suggesting that her cooking is a 'design' (line 14) – an English term that might appear in a casual (chiTonga) conversation among adults but is unlikely to be used neutrally by a young girl like Lushomo. Rather than elaborating on her cooking job, Lushomo seems interested in displaying her own proficiency in English, thereby implicitly challenging Mutinta's critique. As a response to this, Talala questions Lushomo's use of this term, asking 'Is there any *design* in cooking?' (line 15). This question is left unanswered, but Mutinta seems to regain her position at the end of the extract by challenging Sinyimbwe's classification of the cooking as a 'town way' (line 18).

Conclusion

With its formalised practices and connotations to modernity and the West, the school carried great symbolic power in a society nurturing collective dreams of a more comfortable and secure existence. People might have seen too many youngsters return empty-handed from college and secondary school to engage fully in their children's schooling, but they remained invested in the idea of modern education, giving them a sense of hope and dignity in an ambiguous moral landscape. This might include the use of writing and conceptual language, like the 'method' or 'design of cooking', the 'science of a bicycle', or the 'system of farming', positioning both oneself and fellow participants against ideas of expertise, modernity and social success. Such applicable use of schooling often surpassed its long-term value, which was liable to cause disappointment and failure. Observing adults and older children employ English words and abstract concepts in daily talk, younger children learned that being educated or rather *acting* educated was a legitimate and often very successful strategy for obtaining recognition and power in social situations, both inside and outside of school. Children might share their parents' enthusiasm for the idea of school, but in their tangible interactions and orientations, they generally seemed more concerned with building a place for themselves within the immediate realm of family and peers. As we have seen, children displayed great discursive agency and creativity in this respect, reworking powerful registers and hierarchies for their own purposes that might not be known – or acknowledged – by surrounding society, including the school institution itself.

Notes

1. Khama and I made this recording while observing from the back of the classroom. English is marked with bold.
2. This recording was made one night in mid January 2009, when the new school year at Mbabala Basic had just begun. The family recorded themselves, and apart from Lila, Levias, Luyando and Oscar, 7-year-old Calleen was also present.
3. As per usual, I had asked the women permission to record and, in the case above, observe them while they were talking, just as I had told them to speak freely and not try to accommodate with Khama or me. As appears in this extract, however, conversations would often reflect the presence of me and/or the recorder, centering, at least initially, around me, the research project or more generally about education and 'life in the West'.
4. This recording was made by the Mweemba family themselves.
5. On the day of recording the conversation above, Khama and I had visited the family's homestead, conducting interviews and requesting the family to record themselves that same night. When we first arrived around 2 PM, I greeted the family members present by saying *Mwalibizya buti*, the chiTonga phrase for 'Good afternoon'. Alfred answered me in English, saying 'Good evening', as noted by Roy above (line 9). Having been subject to the family's linguistic corrections of my chiTonga numerous times, I jokingly told Alfred that he ought to say 'Good afternoon', rather than 'Good evening'.
6. An earlier version of the subsequent analyses was published in the article Clemensen (2015).

🌿 Conclusion

Past and Future Perspectives

When I grow up I would like to be a teacher.
—Choolwe, 14-year-old boy at Mbabala Basic School

Nowadays are bad years, very bad years.
—Benson, 82-year-old former headman, father and grandfather of 28 children

Since my main stay in Hang'ombe in 2008–2009, the children appearing in this book have become teenagers and young adults, some having had children of their own, some having left Hang'ombe for work, marriage, further schooling or other life circumstances. Except for a brief revisit in 2010, I have not managed to maintain much direct contact with members of the four families, but Khama and I have kept in touch through regular e-mails, allowing me to stay informed especially about his close family members. Their recent trajectories reflect the volatility and close interdependence marking many villagers' lives: in September 2015, Khama's 89-year-old father Benson died in a road accident, forcing his wife (Khama's mother) Sarah, his daughter (Khama's sister) Minivah and her five children – Talala, Mududu, Lushomo, Habeenzu and Lweendo – to leave their land, livestock and houses to some of Benson's relatives, who claimed entitlement to all his former possessions and were granted them by local authorities. As I write this in early 2019, 21-year-old Talala and 13-year-old Habeenzu are living with their grandmother Sarah and her extended relatives in the rural area of Batoka, about 60 km east of Hang'ombe. Habeenzu is in grade six at the local school, while Talala completed grade twelve in 2013 and is currently preparing for a re-exam in certain subjects to qualify for college, preferably nursing or teaching. She works at a hairdresser while taking care of her 3-year-old son. 19-year-old Mududu and 10-year-old Lweendo both live with their mother Minivah in a small house in Mbabala Township, assisting her with the sale of garden vegetables at the local market. In 2012, Mududu entered secondary school in the town of Monze but had to leave after grade ten when she got pregnant and return to her mother's home. She is now saving money to enter Mbabala Secondary School, which opened in early 2018. 10-year-old Lweendo is not yet in school as Minivah needs her assistance at the market and finds it difficult to pay her school fees. 18-year-old Lushomo lives with her 1-year-old baby by her uncle Claude and his family in the town of Chipata in Zambia's eastern province. She left grade nine prematurely due to her pregnancy but hopes to proceed with her studies later this year with Claude's support.

Khama himself now lives with his wife and two daughters in Harare, Zimbabwe, teaching and finishing his PhD in Linguistics at the local university while trying to support his nieces and nephews' schooling. From the Phiri homestead, Khama told me that Julu left grade six to herd his own cattle, while Senefa is currently in grade five. Flora left school in grade seven and later had a number of children. From the Mweemba homestead, Disteria is currently in grade nine, while her brother Munsanje had to leave school in grade four as his parents could no longer pay his school fees. From the Hambuulo homestead, 19-year-old Luyando recently had a baby but is currently finishing grade eight at Mbabala Secondary School. Her older sister Chipo, who was finishing secondary school during my stay in Hang'ombe, got married right after grade twelve and now lives in a neighbouring village. Luyando's brothers Calleen and Oscar are both studying at Mbabala Secondary School, doing grade 10 and 12 respectively.

Many of the children presented in this study have thus remained invested in schooling one way or another, but they have also faced the challenges of balancing school requirements with other concerns. According to Khama's recent updates, especially many of the girls seem to be struggling with this balance, taking care of their young babies – mostly alone or with limited support from the babies' fathers, who themselves rely on their parents and relatives – while hoping or planning to return to school when or if their circumstances eventually improve. Benson's death and his relatives' occupation of his land and possessions clearly impaired his grandchildren's continued schooling – especially 10-year-old Lweendo, who rather than going to school like most of her peers and her older siblings at that age now assists her mother in growing and selling vegetables. But although their case may seem particularly grave, experiences of sudden upheaval continue to be the norm rather than the exception among villagers, as their level of social and material security has generally remained very low.

As noted in the introduction, such profound uncertainty can be viewed as a basic living condition in many parts of contemporary Africa, requiring a high level of adaptability for both males and females of all ages (Cooper and Pratten 2015; Haram and Yamba 2009). To outside observers – perhaps especially those living in relatively secure and affluent societies in the Western hemisphere – some of the social conduct depicted in this book may appear dubious, like adults drinking, stealing or prostituting themselves while living within the range of prying neighbours. But as responses to fluctuating harvest results and periodical starvation, occasional theft or prostitution might serve to feed oneself and one's family, just as alcohol might alleviate the pressures of hard labour and a precarious future, if only momentarily. To some (Western middle-class) readers, the parents in this book might appear somewhat careless in letting their young children move freely around the community, unprotected against the moral ambiguities they might meet. But in family economies relying heavily on the joint work effort of all members and children's early maturity and self-sustenance, shielding them from the concerns and ambiguities of adult existence makes little sense. Likewise, many villagers' tendency to maintain a high-flown moral discourse in everyday talk, promoting the goodness of bible reading or schooling, might seem contradictory when they struggle to abide by it and neither the church nor the school seem to improve their living conditions or secure their children's futures. But in the face of pervasive social and economic uncertainty, the symbolic maintenance of clear moral guidelines and institutions may provide merit and motivation in a region still marked by what anthropologist James Ferguson has described as 'not only an economic crisis but a crisis of meaning, in which the way that people are able to understand their experience and to imbue it with significance and dignity has (for many) been dramatically eroded' (Ferguson 1999: 14).

While Zambia's national economy has improved since 2000, subsistence farmers in Southern Province villages like Hang'ombe have experienced little economic progress, as government subsidies have remained sparse and industrial farms and increasing fertiliser prices have impeded the moderate profits they might make on livestock and maize (Resnick and Thurlow 2014). Some have managed to utilise the new market conditions, for example, by repairing mobile phones, taking temporary low-paying jobs in the building industry or buying cheap household articles in Livingstone or Lusaka and selling them in small shops at the local market. But many are deeply disillusioned by their seeming lack of opportunities and the government's inability or unwillingness to improve their living conditions and create regular jobs for them and their children. Historian Kenneth P. Vickery describes how the Plateau Tongas have been known as proficient peasants and cattle-herders at least since the arrival of British colonisers in the 1880s, a proficiency they – unlike many of their neighbouring tribal groupings who were harshly debilitated by the colonisers' forced labour migration – managed to enhance in the subsequent decades of colonisation through a mixture of luck, thrift and ingenuity; for example, by gaining access to fertile land, increasing the number of cattle, and by women actively involving themselves in practically all aspects of cultivating gardens and fields (Vickery 2007: 92ff). From the 1930s, the increasing European control of African maize production gradually curbed the number of subsistence farmers on the Plateaus, favouring white farmers' large-scale production, having settled in the area (ibid.: 100ff). Like other Zambians, the Tongas experienced the euphoria of Independence in 1964 and the country's rapid economic and infrastructural development due to the global demand on copper in the 1960s and early 1970s, along with the devastating economic downfall of the mid 1970s copper crisis, forcing many young rural men to relocate, leaving their families behind for more prosperous work in the mines (Ferguson 1999). But the most enduring crisis experienced by the Plateau Tongas might be the loss of agricultural prosperity, even if this loss began before most of Hang'ombe's current members were born. During one of our many interviews, Khama's by then 82-year-old father Benson told me about his and hundreds of other families' forced resettlement in 1917 when white farmers took over their lands in the area of Pemba, about 50 km west of Hang'ombe. Although this entailed some turbulent years, Benson underlined the fortune of his family and others in gaining larger and better land in the Hang'ombe area; Pemba land had been more sandy and difficult to cultivate. Born in 1926, Benson described the last two decades of farming – from the late 1980s to 2008 – as 'the worst' he had ever experienced, a situation he ascribed to a mixture of increasingly unstable rains, population growth, cattle disease and political incompetence:

> Back then [after resettlement in 1917], we were very few people. So when someone came here to settle, he would possess as much land as possible. And this was good land, fertile land. Even when we got Independence [in 1964], there was plenty of land and livestock to share with one's children

and grandchildren. We had enough rains, normal rains. There were no excess of rains and we had fertiliser, so we never starved back when the years were good. Nowadays, you find there is less land for more people, you don't have fertiliser, the fields are dried up, and most of the cattle is gone, so people are starving. And even when you look at the government, it is a very bad government because it doesn't pay attention to farming. Nowadays are bad years, very bad years.

In 2008–9, few villagers were old enough themselves to have witnessed the 'good years' (*myaaka mibotu*) Benson talked about. The experience of increasing poverty, agricultural and moral decline prevailed across Hang'ombe homesteads and informed much of adults' talk during meals and around the fire at night. While the school offered slight hopes for their children's futures, most parents maintained a pragmatic scepticism towards any ideas of progress and sought to prepare children for a rural adult existence equally precarious to their own. As we have seen, this preparation entailed children's active involvement in practically all adult work chores in households, fields and gardens, where they acquired key insights and procedures through weeks and months of observation, imitation and gradual participation. On a broader scale, this learning practice sustained not only the lives and identities of individual children and families but also the reproduction of a cultural system comprising homesteads, lineages and the entire chiTonga-speaking community. As acknowledged members and contributors to this system, children were offered strong experiences of purpose and belonging, along with possibilities of influence and change. Their relatively broad freedom of movement across the community allowed them to observe and experiment with different aspects of adult life with little adult intervention. Among their siblings and kin of a wide age-span, with whom they spent practically all their out-of-school time, children would process the complex social and linguistic information available to them through playful experiments and transformations of existing power structures. This included concepts and registers of school, whose symbolic power children would utilise to assert themselves among peers, sometimes subverting prevailing age hierarchies.

Compared to children spending most of their waking hours under close adult supervision, as has become the norm among the Western middle-class, children in rural majority societies like Hang'ombe may develop an advanced social maturity and communicative competence through their relative freedom of movement, their early integration in adults' work lives and their constant, unmonitored interactions with younger and older peers. The ability to interpret and creatively use complex social information without much adult guidance might help them navigate and eventually sustain themselves in a society requiring quick and frequent readjustments to ever-changing social, economic, political and climatic circumstances.

Such abilities, however, tend to gain little recognition or stimulation in Zambia's current school system, where rural children are generally perceived as deficient due to their (alleged) lacking English proficiency and ability to answer prefixed, decontextualised questions from adults. As many language education scholars have pointed out, such deficit understandings of minoritised children and their families are highly problematic, as they impede children's schooling and ignore the rich academic potential of their linguistic and discursive repertoires (Avineri et al. 2015; Hornberger and McKay 2010). Using this potential may require extensive changes to existing educational policies and societal norms of schooling, the latter of which are often supported by the same minoritised families and communities facing the greatest challenges in national school systems. As language socialisation scholar Shirley Brice Heath writes,

> research of linguistic anthropologists showing the high variation found in language input behaviors around the world has had little or no effect on either teacher education programs or reading curricula, even as school populations have increasingly diversified from the 1990s forward. Academic research alone cannot alter economic realities or political will. What scholars in linguistic anthropology and other fields willing to take up a long-term perspective *can* do is insistently push against searches for simple solutions. (Heath 2015, emphasis in original)

In rural Zambia, as in any other part of the world, such a long-term perspective on schooling would entail a deeper understanding of children's educational and communicative practices in their home environments, not only in terms of English vs. chiTonga but also of how they interact with others and participate in the world around them. Among Hang'ombe children, this includes quiet and vigilant observations of adults' physical and discursive practices in context along with relatively undisturbed interactions with peers, neither of which are drawn upon in current school programmes. A long-term perspective might also entail an understanding of the school's wider social and symbolic implications in local communities, as provided in this book. In line with language socialisation scholars studying educational access for minoritised students in both Western and majority settings, I call for 'pedagogies that actively sustain the cultural and linguistic competence of nondominant students' families and communities, while offering "access to dominant cultural competence"' (Paris 2012, cited in McCarty 2015: 72). In Zambia and other sub-Saharan countries, this would entail more extensive research on children's social and linguistic communities – especially in rural areas – in terms of wider political and economic changes and the increasing significance of mediated discourse on TV and social media. Language socialisation studies offer a powerful analytical framework in this respect, combining close linguistic-ethnographic analysis of children and their interlocutors in their everyday surroundings with reflections on broader social reproduction and change.

Inspired by recent calls for more nuanced depictions of African children (Abebe and Ofosu-Kusi 2016), I have sought to neither victimise nor romanticise children's lives and learning paths in Hang'ombe Village. Obviously, the extracts and analyses in this book cannot provide an all-encompassing view, but I hope they may counter widespread stereotypes and inspire more genuine inquiry into the voices and perspectives of children in many different regions and environments in contemporary Africa.

🌿 References

Abebe, T., and Y. Ofosu-Kusi. 2016. 'Beyond Pluralizing African Childhoods: Introduction', *Childhood* 23(3): 303–16.

Abrahams, R.D. 1974. 'Black Talking on the Streets', in R. Bauman and J. Sherzer (eds), *Explorations in the Ethnography of Speaking*. Cambridge: Cambridge University Press, pp. 337–73.

Alber, E., S. Van der Geest and S. Reynolds Whyte. 2008. *Generations in Africa: Connections and Conflicts*. Berlin: Lit Verlag.

Alidou, H. et al. 2006. *Optimizing Learning and Education in Africa: The Language Factor*. Paris: Unesco.

Avineri, N., and E. Johnson. 2015. 'Introduction', *Journal of Linguistic Anthropology* 25(1): 67–68.

Avineri, N. et al. 2015. 'Invited Forum: Bridging the "Language Gap"', *Journal of Linguistic Anthropology* 25(1): 66–86.

Baquedano-López, P., and S. Kattan. 2008. 'Language Socialization in Schools', in P.A. Duff and N.H. Hornberger (eds), *Encyclopedia of Language and Education: Language Socialization*. New York: Springer, pp. 161–73.

Bernstein, B. 1973. *Class, Codes and Control*. London: Routledge & K. Paul.

Bloch, M. 1989. 'Young Boys' and Girls' Play at Home and in the Community: A Cultural-Ecological Framework', in M.N. Bloch and A.D. Pellegrini (eds), *The Ecological Context of Children's Play*. Norwood, NJ: Ablex.

Blum-Kulka, S., D. Huck-Taglicht and H. Avni. 2004. 'The Social and Discursive Spectrum of Peer Talk', *Discourse Studies* 6(3): 291–306.

Borchgrevink, A. 2003. 'Silencing Language: Of Anthropologists and Interpreters', *Ethnography* 4(1): 95–121.

Brock-Utne, B., Z. Desai and M. Qorro. 2006. *Focus on Fresh Data on the Language of Instruction Debate in Tanzania and South Africa*. Cape Town: African Minds.

Bucholtz, M. 2000. 'The Politics of Transcription', *Journal of Pragmatics* 32(10): 1439–65.

Cazden, C.B. 2001. *Classroom Discourse: The Language of Teaching and Learning*. Portsmouth, NH: Heinemann.

Cekaite, A. et al. 2014. *Children's Peer Talk: Learning from Each Other*. Cambridge: Cambridge University Press.

Christiansen, C., M. Utas and H.E. Vigh. 2006. *Navigating Youth, Generating Adulthood: Social Becoming in an African Context*. Uppsala: Nordiska Afrikainstitutet.

Clemensen, N. 2010. 'Teaching in a Language Limbo: Zambian Primary Teachers Caught between Policy and Reality', in P. Cuvelier et al. (eds), *Multilingualism from Below*. Hatfield, South Africa: Van Schaik, pp. 35–50.

———. 2015. 'Staging an Educated Self: Linguistic Displays of Schooling among Rural Zambian Children', *Anthropology and Education Quarterly* 46(3): 244–59.

———. 2016. 'Exploring Ambiguous Realms: Access, Exposure and Agency in the Interactions of Rural Zambian Children', *Childhood* 23(3): 317–32.

Cliggett, L. 2000. 'Gendered Support Strategies of the Elderly in the Gwembe Valley, Zambia', in C. Lancaster and K.P. Vickery (eds), *The Tonga-Speaking Peoples of Zambia and Zimbabwe: Essays in Honor of Elizabeth Colson*. University Press of America, pp. 219–36.

———. 2001. 'Survival Strategies of the Elderly in Gwembe Valley, Zambia: Gender, Residence and Kin Networks', *Journal of Cross-cultural Gerontology* 16(4): 309–32.

———. 2003. 'Male Wealth and Claims to Motherhood: Gendered Resource Access and Intergenerational Relations in Gwembe Valley, Zambia', in G. Clark (ed.), *Gender at Work in Economic Life*. Walnut Creek, CA: Altamira Press, pp. 207–23.

———. 2005. *Grains from Grass: Aging, Gender, and Famine in rural Africa*. Ithaca, NY: Cornell University Press.

Cliggett, L. et al. 2007. 'Chronic Uncertainty and Momentary Opportunity: A Half Century of Adaptation among Zambia's Gwembe Tonga', *Human Ecology* 35(1): 19–31.

Cooper, E., and D. Pratten (eds). 2015. *Ethnographies of Uncertainty in Africa*. New York: Palgrave Macmillan.

Corsaro, W.A. 2009. 'Peer Culture', in J. Qvortrup, W.A. Corsaro and M.-S. Honig (eds), *The Palgrave Handbook of Childhood Studies*. Hampshire: Palgrave Macmillan, pp. 301–15.

Crehan, K. 1997. *The Fractured Community: Landscapes of Power and Gender in Rural Zambia*. Berkeley: University of California Press.

De León, L. 2007. 'Parallelism, Metalinguistic Play, and the Interactive Emergence of Zinacantec Mayan Siblings' Culture', *Research on Language and Social Interaction* 40(4): 405–36.

———. 2009. 'Between Frogs and Black-Winged Monkeys: Orality, Evidentials, and Authorship in Tzotzil (Mayan) Children's Narratives', in J. Guo et al. (eds), *Crosslinguistic Approaches to the Psychology of Language: Research in the Tradition of Dan Isaac Slobin*. New York: Psychology Press, pp. 175–92.

———. 2015. 'Mayan Children's Creation of Learning Ecologies by Initiative and Co-operative actions', in R. Mejia-Arauz, M. Correa-Chávez and B. Rogoff (eds), *Children Learn by Observing and Contributing to Family and Community Endeavors: A Cultural Paradigm. Advances in Child Development and Behaviour*. Waltham, MA: Academic Press, pp. 153–180.

———. 2018. 'Playing at Being Bilingual: Bilingual Performances, Stance, and Language Scaling in Mayan Tzotzil Siblings' Play', *Journal of Pragmatics* 144: 92–108.

Duranti, A. 1997. *Linguistic Anthropology*. Cambridge: Cambridge University Press.

Ensor, M.O. 2012. *African Childhoods: Education, Development, Peacebuilding, and the Youngest Continent*. New York: Palgrave Macmillan.

Evaldsson, A.-C. 2005. 'Staging Insults and Mobilizing Categorizations in a Multiethnic Peer Group', *Discourse and Society* 16(6): 763–86.

———. 2009. 'Play and Games', in J. Qvortrup, W.A. Corsaro and M.-S. Honig (eds), *The Palgrave Handbook of Childhood Studies*. Hampshire: Palgrave Macmillan, pp. 316–27.

Evans, J.L. 1994. *Childrearing Practices in Sub-Saharan Africa: An Introduction to the Studies*. Toronto: ECCD.

Evans-Pritchard, E.E. 1951. *Social Anthropology*. London: Cohen and West.

Ferguson, J. 1999. *Expectations of Modernity: Myths and Meanings of Urban Life on the Zambian Copperbelt*. Berkeley: University of California Press.

Figueroa, A.M., and P. Baquedano-López. 2017. 'Language Socialization and Schooling', in P. Duff and S. May (eds), *Encyclopedia of Language and Education 10: Language Socialization*, 3rd edn. Cham, Switzerland: Springer, pp. 141–53.

Friedl, E. 2004. 'The Ethnography of Children', *Iranian Studies* 37(4): 655–63.

Geissler, P.W., and R.J. Prince. 2004. 'Shared Lives: Exploring Practices of Amity between Grandmothers and Grandchildren in Western Kenya', *Africa: Journal of the International African Institute* 74(1): 95–120.

Geschiere, P. 2013. *Witchcraft, Intimacy and Trust: Africa in Comparison*. Chicago: The University of Chicago Press.

Goffman, E. 1967. *Interaction Ritual: Essays in Face to Face Behavior*. Garden City, NY: Doubleday.

Goldman, L.R. 1998. *Child's Play: Myth, Mimesis, and Make-Believe*. New York: Oxford University Press.

Goodwin, M.H., and A. Kyratzis. 2012. 'Peer Language Socialization', in A. Duranti, E. Ochs and B.B. Schieffelin (eds), *The Handbook of Language Socialization*. Malden, MA: Wiley-Blackwell, pp. 365–90.

Haddad, C. 2008. *Improving the Quality of Mother Tongue-based Literacy and Learning: Case Studies from Asia, Africa and South America*. Paris: Unesco.

Hansen, K.T. 2005. 'Getting Stuck in the Compound: Some Odds against Social Adulthood in Lusaka, Zambia', *Africa Today* 51(4): 3–16.

Haram, L., and C.B. Yamba. 2009. *Dealing with Uncertainty in Contemporary African Lives*. Uppsala: Nordiska Afrikainstitutet.

Harkness, S., and C.M. Super. 1992. 'Parental Ethnotheories in Action', in I.E. Sigel et al. *Parental Belief Systems: The Psychological Consequences for Children*, 2nd edn. New York: Lawrence Erlbaum Associates, pp. 373–92.

Harkness, S. et al. 2010. 'Parental Ethnotheories of Children's Learning', in D.F. Lancy, J. Bock and S. Gaskins (eds), *The Anthropology of Learning in Childhood*. Lanham, MD: AltaMira Press, pp. 65–81.

Heath, S.B. 1983. *Ways with Words: Language, Life, and Work in Communities and Classrooms*. Cambridge: Cambridge University Press.

———. 2015. 'The Simple and Direct? Almost Never the Solution', *Journal of Linguistic Anthropology* 25(1): 68–70.

Heugh, K. 2009. 'Literacy and Bi/Multilingual Education in Africa', in T. Skutnabb-Kangas et al. (eds), *Multilingual Education for Social Justice*. Bristol: Multilingual Matters, pp. 103–24.

Honwana, A.M., and F. De Boeck (eds). 2005. *Makers and Breakers: Children and Youth in Postcolonial Africa*. Oxford: James Currey.

Hornberger, N., and S. Lee McKay (eds). 2010. *Sociolinguistics and Language Education*. Toronto: Multilingual Matters.

Howard, K. 2007. 'Kinterm Usage and Hierarchy in Thai Children's Peer Groups', *Journal of Linguistic Anthropology* 17(2): 204–31.

———. 2009a. 'Breaking in and Spinning Out: Repetition and Decalibration in Thai Children's Play Genres', *Language in Society* 38(3): 339–63.

———. 2009b. '"When Meeting Mrs. Teacher, Each Time We Should Show Respect": Standardizing Respect and Politeness in a Northern Thai Classroom', *Linguistics and Education* 20(3): 254–72.

Hymes, D. 1967. 'Why Linguistics Need the Sociologist', *Social Research* 34(4): 632–47.

Imoh, A.T.-D. 2016. 'From the Singular to the Plural: Exploring Diversities in Contemporary Childhoods in Sub-Saharan Africa', *Childhood* 23(3): 455–68.

James, A., and A. Prout. 1997. *Constructing and Reconstructing Childhood: Contemporary Issues in the Sociological Study of Childhood*, 2nd edn. London: Falmer Press.

Jirata, T.J. 2012. 'Learning through Play: An Ethnographic Study of Children's Riddling in Ethiopia', *Africa* 82(2): 272–86.

Johnson-Hanks, J. 2006. *Uncertain Honor: Modern Motherhood in an African Crisis*. Chicago: University of Chicago Press.

Kampmann, J. 2006. 'Etiske overvejelser i etnografisk børneforskning', in E. Gulløv and S. Højlund (eds), *Feltarbejde blandt børn: Metodologi og etik i etnografisk børneforskning*. Copenhagen: Gyldendal, pp. 167–83.

Katz, C. 2004. *Growing up Global: Economic Restructuring and Children's Everyday Lives*. Minneapolis: University of Minnesota Press.

———. 2012. 'Work and Play: Economic Restructuring and Children's Everyday Lives in Rural Sudan', in G. Spittler and M.F.C. Bourdillon (eds), *African Children at Work: Working and Learning in Growing up for Life*. Berlin: LIT Verlag, pp. 227–48.

Kochman, T. 1983. 'The Boundary between Play and Non-play in Black Duelling', *Language in Society* 12: 329–37.

Kulick, D., and B.B. Schieffelin. 2004. 'Language Socialization', in A. Duranti (ed.), *A Companion to Linguistic Anthropology*. Malden, MA: Blackwell Publishing, pp. 349–68.

Kyratzis, A. 2007. 'Using the Social Organizational Affordances of Pretend Play in American Preschool Girls' Interactions', *Research on Language and Social Interaction* 40(4): 321–52.

Labov, W. 1972. *Language in the Inner City: Studies in the Black English Vernacular*. Philadelphia: University of Pennsylvania.

Lancaster, C., and K.P. Vickery. 2007. *The Tonga-Speaking Peoples of Zambia and Zimbabwe: Essays in Honor of Elizabeth Colson*. Lanham, MD: University Press of America.

Lancy, D.F. 1996. *Playing on the Mother-Ground: Cultural Routines for Children's Development*. New York: The Guildford Press.

———. 2015. *The Anthropology of Childhood: Cherubs, Chattel, Changelings*, 2nd edn. Cambridge: Cambridge University Press.

Marcus, G.E. 1995. 'Ethnography in/of the World System: The Emergence of Multi-Sited Ethnography', *Annual Review of Anthropology* 24: 95–117.

McCarty, T.L. 2015. 'How the Logic of Gap Discourse Perpetuates Education Inequality: A View from the Ethnography of Language Policy', *Journal of Linguistic Anthropology* 25(1): 70–72.

Mead, M. 1928. *Coming of Age in Samoa: A Psychological Study of Primitive Youth for Western Civilisation*. New York: Perennial Classics.

Minks, A. 2006. 'Mediated Intertextuality in Pretend Play among Nicaraguan Miskitu Children', *Texas Linguistic Forum* 49: 117–27.

———. 2008. 'Performing Gender in Song Games among Nicaraguan Miskitu Children', *Language and Communication* 28: 36–56.

———. 2010. 'Socializing Heteroglossia among Miskitu Children on the Caribbean Coast of Nicaragua', *Pragmatics* 4: 495–522.

———. 2013. *Voices of Play: Miskitu Children's Speech and Song on the Atlantic Coast of Nicaragua*. First Peoples: New Directions in Indigenous Studies Series. Tucson: University of Arizona Press.

Mizinga, F.M. 2000. 'Marriage and Bridewealth in a Matrilineal Society: The Case of the Tonga of Southern Zambia: 1900–1996', *African Economic History* 28: 53–87.

Moore, H.L., and M. Vaughan. 1994. *Cutting down Trees: Gender, Nutrition, and Agricultural Change in the Northern Province of Zambia, 1890–1990*. Portsmouth: Heinemann.

Moore, L.C. 1999. 'Language Socialization Research and French Language Education in Africa: A Cameroonian Case Study', *The Canadian Modern Language Review* 56(2): 329–50.

———. 2009. 'On Communicative Competence … in the Field', *Language and Communication* 29(3): 244–54.

Nájera, F.L. 2009. 'Los directivos en la organizacion social del grupo de pares de ninos bilingues de San Isidro Buensuceso, Tlaxcala: Un enfoque interactivo', *Maestria en Linguistica Indoamericana*. CIESAS, Mexico.

Nsamenang, A.B. 1992. *Human Development in Cultural Context: A Third World Perspective*. Cross-Cultural Research and Methodology Series, vol. 16. London: Sage.

———. 2008. 'Agency in Early Childhood Learning and Development in Cameroon', *Contemporary Issues in Early Childhood* 9(3): 211–23.

Nsamenang, A.B., and M.E. Lamb. 1994. 'Socialisation of Nso Children in the Bamenda Grassfields of Northwest Cameroon', in P.M. Greenfield and R.R. Cocking (eds), *Cross-Cultural Roots of Minority Child Development*. New York: Psychology Press, pp. 133–46.

Paris, D. 2012. 'Culturally Sustaining Pedagogy: A Needed Change in Stance, Terminology, and Practice', *Educational Researcher* 41(2): 93–97.

Paugh, A.L. 2005. 'Multilingual Play: Children's Code-Switching, Role Play, and Agency in Dominica, West Indies', *Language in Society* 34(1): 63–86.

─────. 2012. *Playing with Languages: Children and Change in a Caribbean Village*. New York: Berghahn.

Posner, D. 2005. *Institutions and Ethnic Politics in Africa*. Cambridge: Cambridge University Press.

Qvortrup, J., W.A. Corsaro and M.-S. Honig (eds). 2009. *The Palgrave Handbook of Childhood Studies*. Houndmills: Palgrave Macmillan.

Resnick, D., and J. Thurlow. 2014. 'The Political Economy of Zambia's Recovery: Structural Change without Transformation?' Discussion paper. International Food Policy Research Institute (IFPRI), Development Strategy and Governance Division.

Reynolds, J. 2007. '"Buenos días/((military salute))": The Natural History of a Coined Insult', *Research on Language and Social Interaction* 40(4): 437–65.

─────. 2010. 'Enregistering the Voices of Discursive Figures of Authority in Antonero Children's Socio-dramatic Play', *Pragmatics* 4: 467–93.

─────. 2013. 'Refracting Articulations of Citizenship, Delicuencia and Vigilantism in Boys' Sociodramatic Play in Postwar Guatemala', *Language and Communication* 33: 515–31.

Rindstedt, C. 2001. 'Quichua Children and Language Shift in an Andean Community: School, Play and Sibling Caretaking', Unpublished dissertation. Department of Child Studies, Linköping University.

Rindstedt, C., and K. Aronsson. 2002. 'Growing up Monolingual in a Bilingual Community: The Quichua Revitalization Paradox', *Language in Society* 31: 721–42.

Rogoff, B. 2014. 'Learning by Observing and Pitching in to Family and Community Endeavors: An Orientation', *Human Development* 57: 69–81.

Rogoff, B. et al. 2003. 'Firsthand Learning through Intent Participation', *Annual Review of Psychology* 54: 175–203.

Sampa, F.K. 2003. 'Country Case Study, Republic of Zambia: Primary Reading Programme (PRP): Improving Access and Quality Education in Basic Schools'. Paper presented at the ADEA Biennial Meeting.

─────. 2005. *Zambia's Primary Reading Programme (PRP): Improving Access and Quality Education in Basic Schools*. Paris: ADEA.

Schieffelin, B.B., and E. Ochs. 1986. *Language Socialization across Cultures*. Cambridge: Cambridge University Press.

Serpell, R. 1993. *The Significance of Schooling: Life-journeys in an African Society*. Cambridge: Cambridge University Press.

Spitulnik, D. 1998. 'The Production of Language Ideologies in Zambian Broadcasting', in B.B. Schieffelin, K.A. Woolard and P.V. Kroskrity (eds), *Language Ideologies: Practice and Theory*. New York: Oxford University Press.

Spittler, G., and M. Bourdillon (eds). 2012. *African Children at Work: Working and Learning in Growing up for Life*. Berlin: LIT Verlag.

Stambach, A. 2000. *Lessons from Kilimanjaro: Schooling, Community and Gender in East Africa*. New York: Routledge.

Super, C.M., and S. Harkness. 2008. 'Globalization and its Discontents: Challenges to Developmental Theory and Practice in Africa', *International Journal of Psychology* 43(2): 107–13.

Thorne, B. 1993. *Gender Play: Girls and Boys in School.* New Brunswick, NJ: Rutgers University Press.

Toren, C. 1993. 'Making History: The Significance of Childhood Cognition for a Comparative Anthropology of Mind', *Man* 28(3): 461–78.

Unesco. 2000. *2015 Millennium Development Goals.* Paris: Unesco.

——— . 2012. *Education for All: Global Monitoring Report 2012: Youth and Skills: Putting Education to Work.* Paris: Unesco.

Vickery, K.P. 2007. 'The Emergence of a Plateau Tonga Peasantry: Economic Change, 1890–1940', in C. Lancaster and K.P. Vickery (eds), *The Tonga-Speaking Peoples of Zambia and Zimbabwe: Essays in Honor of Elizabeth Colson.* University Press of America, pp. 83–106.

Whiteley, W.H. (ed.). 2018. *Language Use and Social Change: Problems of Multilingualism with Special Reference to Eastern Africa*, 2nd edn. Oxford: International African Institute.

Whiting, B.B., and John W.M. Whiting. 1975. *Children of Six Cultures: A Psycho-cultural Analysis.* Cambridge: Harvard University Press.

Whyte, S.R., and G. Siu. 2015. 'Contingency: Interpersonal and Historical Dependencies in HIV Care', in E. Cooper and D. Pratten (eds), *Ethnographies of Uncertainty in Africa.* New York: Palgrave Macmillan, pp. 19–35.

World Bank. 2013. 'Zambia's Job Challenge: Realities on the Ground', *Zambia Economic Brief* (2). Washington, DC: World Bank.

Zambian Ministry of Education. 1996. *Educating our Future: National Policy on Education.* Lusaka: Ministry of Education.

🌿 Index

* 9 7 8 1 8 0 0 7 3 4 3 2 6 *